Confessions of a Glommer

Independence, Indifference, and Love

by Lee Marie Schnebly

Copyright 2013 by Lee Marie Schnebly
All Rights Reserved

First Edition

No part of this book may be produced or utilized in
any form by any means, electronic or mechanical,
including photocopying, recording or by
any information storage and retrieval system,
without permission in writing from the publisher.

Published by: Cider Press
2641 N. Arcadia Avenue
Tucson, AZ 85712 / USA

ISBN: 0930831071
ISBN 13: 9780930831073

Cover Design: Al Gyuro
Editing: Sedona Heidinger
and Laurie Schnebly

To order additional copies, contact
address above or Lee Schnebly
at TucsonLeona@gmail.com

To my fellow glommers

and our beloved non-glommers

Contents

One: What's a Glommer?	1
What Goes Into Defining Ourselves?	4
What Are Our Expectations?	7
When Do You Start Being A Glommer?	8
After High School	12
The Prince	14
Two: You Mean We Have Differences?	19
Communication	20
What Does Your Pie Chart Say?	23
The Magic Geranium	26
What Makes You Happy?	29
Three: Making the Choice	39
The Three-Legged Stool	48
Four: Cages	57
Escaping the Cage	65
Five: Another Epiphany	77
Fifteen Years Later	93
Six: You're The Star	97
Seven: Dependencies and Beliefs	113
Eight: Co-Stars and Friends	127

Nine: Enjoy the Music	143
Ten: God	163
Eleven: What Gets in the Way?	177
Twelve: Solutions	187
Thirteen: Intimacy and Beliefs The Final Solution	203 209
Fourteen: How Quickly Can I Make These Changes?	219
Acknowledgments	228
About the Author	230

one

What's a Glommer?

Our daughters coined the word years ago when they noticed that people differ from others in their preferences. "Some people like to glom onto a person and stay really close to them all the time," Laurie explained. "Other people don't ever want to glom onto anybody nor be glommed onto. They'd be called non-glommers."

Immediately I recognized myself as a lifelong glommer. Four seconds later I realized my husband is a lifelong non-glommer, and that difference is at the heart of all our problems. *All* our problems? Virtually every single one.

However, we'll be celebrating our 60th anniversary very soon, and both of us want to continue living together. In spite of disappointments we've experienced, we've gone through many stages in dealing with them. Along the way we've adjusted to the other's ways beyond what we'd have originally have thought possible.

Recently I wondered if "glom" could be a legitimate word, so I looked in <u>Webster's Universal College</u>

Dictionary and found it labeled as slang. "To steal. To catch or grab. To look at. To get hold of."

Offerings in other dictionaries included "To seize, to take by theft, to knock off, to hook, to acquire, to get, and to take possession of."

Oh dear. Not a very complimentary list of verbs, and I suspect they're exactly how a non-glommer sees a glommer. Too clingy.

How does a glommer see a glommer? As one who loves completely. One who is so intensely loving, almost adoring, that one wants to be near the lovee much of the time. A glommer puts the lover on a pedestal and wants to get closer than the pedestal will allow.

A true glommer believes love like that is how life should be, with the two glommers choosing to go and see and do together. What they'd do is unimportant. What is important is that they want to be together, paying attention to each other.

This does not mean, though, that the ideal match would do *everything* together. That would be destructive to our human-ness and most likely the death of the relationship itself. We should each go and see and do all kinds of things separately, enjoying all aspects of life thoroughly unless they involve breaking our rules of morality and ethics.

We'd immerse ourselves in each moment of the various experiences we have apart from one another, knowing that we'd get to be with the lovee again soon. We'd come back together with freshened attitudes, delighted to share hugs and kisses and conversation. *Lots* of conversation.

We'd talk about what we did that day, whom we saw, where we went and how we felt. How we feel now. What we might hope to do tomorrow or next week or next year. We'd share our hopes, dreams and fears and feel comfortably certain we'd be understood.

Does that mean we'd take separate vacations? Sure, why not? He wants to go here, and she wants to go there, and it's a good use of time to do them separately. We'd take plenty of vacations together as well, because enjoying common experiences gives us memories of sharing fun. Sharing fun and sharing non-fun as well.

"Remember when you were passing a car at night and we ran smack into a trailer someone had left on the left side of the road?"

"Yeah. Wow, scary, huh?"

I have a wall hanging that says, "Friendship doubles our joy and divides our grief." Sharing both good things and bad strengthens our bond.

So being a glommer is *not* wanting 100% togetherness. It's how we treat the other person when we are together.

Time together is vital since our feelings go where our energy goes. Let me re-type that in caps since it's so crucial: FEELINGS GO WHERE OUR ENERGY GOES.

If I spend the majority of my daylight hours at a workplace, my job will probably become more important to me as time passes. If I am into playing tennis every other day, my love of tennis will probably increase as my expertise does. If I'm writing books most of the time, it's possible I'll think about the current book more often than I think about my mate.

If I'm totally there for our kids, my love for them will grow more than my love for my mate.

Of course there are exceptions to all of those, but the fact remains that time spent on projects intensifies our interest.

What Goes Into Defining Ourselves?

If we look at personality preferences, we might draw a line with non-glommers at the left end and glommers at the right.

Probably most of us would place ourselves somewhere between the two extremes. None of the positions is right or wrong, none is better or worse. They're all just unconsciously placed so we can enjoy life to the fullest.

The way we enjoy life depends on many things. Some is no doubt in our DNA, and we might recognize Aunt Margie's gift of joke telling in one of our cousins. Kids might be fascinated with sports, music or working on car engines from an early age if someone in their family excels at that. We may choose to pursue the interest or abandon it for other interests, but the basic skill is probably born within us.

Are you an introvert or an extrovert? Whichever you are was probably evident way back when you were a child. Of course we make the decision whether or not we want to develop the behavior of the opposite category, but the roots of either are in place at birth.

Fortunately each of has the opportunity of adjusting our behavior to suit our purposes, and most of us are quite successful at achieving the style we want.

The late psychiatrist Alfred Adler used to encourage his patients to "Act *as if* until it becomes real." A shy person has the ability to put on a manner of confidence and become a social success if he makes the decision to pursue it.

Author M. Scott Skinner said that people are always asking him "What *is* human nature?"

Dr. Skinner answers, "Human nature is pooping in your diaper." We're born that way, so it's clearly our nature.

But in a year or so our mothers get tired of changing diapers, and they train us to go in the potty. We've just changed our human nature! That's only one example of how we change if we have a reason to do so. The reason can stem from our own desire or from society's pressure on us, but it's amazingly effective either way.

Many times, however, we resist changing our nature, even if it might improve our lives in some way. You probably know people who say, "I'm just the kind of person who can't let go of a grudge." I silently think, "You could if you want to," but I rarely say it.

"I'm the kind of person who can't control my temper. It just comes out all by itself." Well, we let it come out, but author Wayne Dyer says this: "If someone were giving you a karate chop every three seconds until you stopped your anger, you'd stop it in no time." Same with tears. "I can't *help* crying," would disappear quickly after the first karate chop.

Blaming our behavior on our nature isn't fair. It's a copout we like to use to allow us to continue our habits, and we generally believe we can't help it, but we clearly can. We might allow ourselves to *say*, "I can't help it; it's just who I am," but we must know in our hearts that we're cheating ourselves. We simply don't have any wish to change or we could.

Can we change our basic makeup, then? Well, no, not in every way. We have brown eyes or blue eyes, and those are the permanent colors of our eyes. We have DNA that makes us lighthearted and jolly or serious and worried, but those traits we *can* affect.

We can change our beliefs, and in so doing, we can change our feelings. If glommers and non-glommers want to be happier together, we have to make some changes for sure.

Okay, one of our options is to break up or get a divorce, an option that many people choose today. "This isn't any fun anymore, and I don't much like this person, so I might as well get a divorce."

We have every right to do that very thing, but it isn't without difficult consequences. I've had many clients over the years who have said (in their second or third marriages), "You know, I think I could have made that first marriage work. I just didn't know it took *work* to have a happy marriage. I thought if I was married and unhappy, I must have an unhappy marriage, and therefore I needed to get out of it."

Sadly, it's so true. People often find themselves hurting in their second marriages as well. And third.

And fourth. And a happy marriage will always evade us unless and until we change our expectations.

What Are Our Expectations?

I fully expected my boyfriend Larry to love me passionately and eagerly forevermore, as I would love him the same way! Once we were married, I knew, we would laugh at everything and have great fun raising our kids together and loving each other as much or probably more than we did in those courting days. I didn't doubt it for a moment.

Falling in love is the giddiest joy we can know, in my opinion. We feel excited, joyous, loving *everybody*, energetic, and positive about almost everything. We explain those magnificent feelings by giving the romance all the credit. "I am *so* so so happy since I've been seeing Larry," I used to think. And it was true.

Interestingly, he was feeling the same way. In fact we used to say, "We feel the same about *everything*, don't we?!" And we'd hold hands and kiss and feel ever so lucky to have found The Person For Whom We Were Meant. We were no doubt the first couple ever who had been this deeply and magically in love. No couple loved like we loved. We believed that with every cell in our bodies. Doubt? It didn't exist.

And in that state of hormonal unbalance and near insanity, when we each saw our loved one walking the earth in an aura of dazzling colored lights, loving us with all his/her heart, we made the most important decision we'd ever made: we married till death do us part, in sickness and in health, yada yada yada.

Did we know I was a glommer and he was a non-glommer? Heck no! Didn't know, didn't care. We had found perfection, so there was no problem.

As news of our engagement spread there were a few warnings from friends, like "Have you talked about your religious beliefs? She's Catholic, and he's Protestant. That could be an issue between you."

We'd smile broadly and say, "Oh, sure, we know there'll be problems, but none we can't handle."

Truth be told, we didn't really think we did or would have problems; at least I didn't, but it seemed only polite that I agree that couples *could*. I had never been happier in my life. I walked on clouds of unbounded joy at having reached the part of my life to which I'd looked forward literally all my life.

When Do You Start Being A Glommer?

Well, I started at age three, when I met my 18-year-old cousin. Bob became my first boyfriend, and I shared that information with everybody around me, including Bob. Somehow I felt I'd been changed by meeting him, and I'd become excited and exciting. I'd reached a level of maturity of feeling special to someone, though I knew full well he wasn't aware I existed.

But who cared? He didn't have to be involved in my love affair with him; it sufficed that I had it all by myself.

And he was The First Crush. We'd met in New York that first time, and I didn't see him again until we visited the same relatives six years later in 1941, just as World War Two was about to become official.

If I'd loved him in civvies, think how I felt seeing him in his Navy uniform. Oh my gosh! I memorized every detail of his uniform, and begged my mother to make me a sailor dress when we got home. (She did, bless her.) Shortly after that Bob was literally blown off the USS *West Virginia* when the Japanese attacked Pearl Harbor. I became his devoted corresponded, sending him cheery missives once a week.

Defending my precocious romantic feelings, I must explain that all Americans were being urged to write our servicemen, keeping up their morale as they fought for our country. We were steeped in military publicity on the radio, in magazines, newspapers, and in glorious movies featuring handsome men in all branches of service.

I lapped it up, the romance of the war. In The Clock, Judy Garland fell in love with Robert Walker, a soldier who was due to ship out the next day, so they had only a few hours to get a license and be married by a justice of the peace. How I wished I could marry Bob. But I could do my part for the USA by writing him frequent cheery letters.

He answered them! Very briefly, but he did care! I think the men overseas would have appreciated even junk mail, but I took his replies as proof of his affection for me. A few years later he sent me pictures of him and his bride! What? He married somebody else? What a jolt *that* was.

But I felt happy for him, and it didn't take very long for me to develop a crush on my brother Paul's best friend, Milton. I was 13, a freshman at Winslow High, where Milton was a senior.

He was in our home often, and if he and Paul were in our living room I'd pick that time to dust the furniture and give any little doodads plenty of polishing and care.

One day my mother said, "Leona, you're a very flirtatious girl. I don't want you hanging around Paul's friends anymore!"

I was shocked and hurt. She was calling me a flirt? *Me*? Of course I wasn't! I was simply in love with Milton. Privately. I sighed, knowing the jig was up, and I had to be someplace else when Milton was around.

To my ecstasy, he invited me to the senior prom. I was thrilled beyond words, and afraid Mama wouldn't let me go, but she did. Winslow was a small town in which everyone knew everyone else. Our fathers worked together on the Santa Fe Railroad. Our mothers were good friends, so Mama knew I'd be safe. After all, he spent many hours in our home.

I needed a formal, and we hadn't the money to buy even fabric for one, but Mrs. Winn, the teacher next door, searched for an old one in her trunk.

It was pink, dusty pink (more from real dust than from its original dye). But it fit, and I wasn't going to argue as long as I got to go at all. Needless to say the prom was a highlight of my life, and the chaste kiss at the door convinced me we were meant to be lifelong lovers!

He had no car, but we walked all over town enjoying each other's company. Paul bought an old Model A for $50, and we'd ride around town with friends almost every evening, singing songs. Milton asked me to go steady in June. I accepted but didn't say much about it at home.

Sadly he was stricken with polio the next month and was sent to the Children's Hospital in Phoenix. Again I was the steady letter writer. I wrote daily. One time his mother took me to see him there, and we stayed a few days in her brother's home.

In the morning we'd take a bus to the hospital and talk to Milton, who was unable to walk so was always in bed. I enjoyed talking to him, but I couldn't help noticing the guy in the bed next to his. Dare Slade was his name. To my shame I found Dare strangely attractive and began to question my love for Milton.

To my credit, though, I continued writing to Milton for many months until he was sent home. In his wheelchair, he was delighted to see me when I'd go over, but the magic was gone. Feeling guilty at the thought of breaking up with him, I struggled with the issue for weeks until I finally did it. He seemed to understand.

(He married someone else, fathered a child and became Winslow's Justice of the Peace.)

I felt a delicious freedom, then, ready to go out with Herbert Keller. Then Claude Ricks. Then Gene Higbee. In each relationship I was madly in love, prone to writing their names as I sat, bored, in class. "Leona Keller." "Mrs. Claude Ricks." "Gene and Leona Higbee." And so on.

I knew that loving a man was the thing I wanted most out of life. Of course I wanted a career, but that would be of much less importance.

Fortunately I was a cradle Catholic who was taught in my formative years that pre-marital sex was a mortal sin, and anyone who indulged in it would surely spend eternity burning in hell. Otherwise I suspect I might have been the most promiscuous girl on Route 66.

I was not alone in my morals, however, because in the forties and fifties girls were all supposed to remain virgins until we married, so boys accepted me as I was. Certainly they tried to talk me out of my scruples, but I was too afraid of the burning in hell part to take the risk. I was a virgin until my honeymoon.

In the meantime I graduated from high school with no desire to go to college. I wanted to go to Pasadena Playhouse in California and become an actress, but we didn't have the money, so it was understood I would work until I earned enough to go.

I became a waitress in Clark's Cafe on Route 66, and I truly loved the work. We could have one free meal a day with anything we wanted except steak. I'd spend the entire morning thinking over the menu and deciding what my meal would be. The shift flew by and I got great tips.

After High School

One day I had a call from a guy named Bill Brennan, a Winslow High graduate several years ahead of me. He needed a pianist to accompany him at a luncheon, and someone had suggested me. We hadn't met, but he came to the house, and guess what. By the end of the hour I was in love with him.

He attended Arizona State College (now Northern Arizona University) in Flagstaff and planned to become an Episcopal priest after graduation. He sang "Night and Day" at the luncheon, and from then on we "went together." He told me about his former girlfriend at college, who happened to be Bette Davis's niece—a girl named Joanne Suckstorff. But I was unconcerned about her.

Now I knew I *must* go to college in Flagstaff to be with my honey! The schoolteacher across the alley from us was an alumna of ASC and talked them into giving me a scholarship, so I was set. Bill and his friends drove me to Flagstaff on the first day, helped me move into the dorm, and went on about their business. Next thing I heard from Bill was, "Hey, Leona. Sorry to tell you this, but I made up with Joanne. Good luck. See ya around."

There I was, at a college in which I had no interest, with no boyfriend. Nothing was left but my exploded dreams. There would be no "Leona Brennan" after all. And I would have made such a good Episcopalian priest's wife.

Ah well. Nothing to do but accept it and enjoy my girlfriends while I kept my eye out for some other boy. I dated a couple of them before I met Mr. Perfect, Eddie Reinig. He was from Queens, NY, spoke like a New Yorker, and had a scar over his left eyebrow, kind of like an exclamation point.

It was love at first sight. We were going steady in no time, and got engaged a year later. I adored him, laughed with him and dreamed with him. I realize now both of us must have been glommers.

Though he, too, was Catholic, he was on the edge of being a juvenile delinquent. He loved to party, sleep with other girls, and dream up ways to find more money, like maybe breaking into the downtown drugstore through the window on the roof. He fascinated me and went along with my morality, finding occasional fun with "the town girls" (Flagstaff girls who lived at home instead of in the dorm).

Needless to say, my mother didn't like him one bit. She told my father not to keep his watch on the piano when Eddie visited, because it might disappear, but I never doubted his honesty.

He graduated a year ahead of me and promptly joined the Air Force, to my horror. While I wrote daily letters, he rarely wrote, and I was devastated at the loss I felt.

The Prince

Some five months after he'd left Flagstaff I got a show at a local radio station, singing and playing the piano. My announcer was a dashing guy named Larry Schnebly, with whom I had my first dinner at Rod's Steak House in Williams. Larry was already a graduate, a DJ, a classy dresser, and he drove a big black Buick with the classic Buick ring on the hood.

We both loved performing. He was president of the drama group and belonged to every club, organization and committee on campus. His manners were impeccable and he kept me laughing besides.

But mostly he loved me. *Now* I had the real Mr. Perfect. My mother thought he was wonderful, and Daddy could once again leave his watch out in the open.

We were all impressed that his grandparents had been among the very first settlers in Sedona, Arizona, and the town had been named for his grandmother, Sedona Schnebly.

This time *his* parents were not all that happy with the relationship, being quite anti-Catholic, but, to their credit, they couldn't have been nicer to me. (Larry told me later that his father had always instructed him: "Don't smoke, don't drink, and stay away from those Catholics!")

By the time I met him he was smoking and drinking, and I realized I was the token Catholic—the last stage of rebellion. But I didn't mind. He was Mr. Perfect, and he loved me.

Our first date had been June 20th, and our wedding was the following June 20th. For most of that year I was teaching first grade in Tucson, while he stayed at his job in Flagstaff. But we wrote letters every day, love letters that assured both of us of our strong, fervent love.

We saw one another maybe five or six times in that period of time; in retrospect not nearly enough to know each other very well.

But with the innocence of youth and the desire of two people in love, we married in total confidence.

Sometimes I wonder what we'd have done if we'd known about glommers and non-glommers. Probably nothing different, since we were so sure we were a perfect match. We'd have said something like, "Oh, sure we have different expectations of marriage, but it won't be anything we can't handle."

As I look back at our courtship, however, I see our leanings clear as day. Like the time he wanted me to see the north rim of the Grand Canyon, so we planned a day trip on a Sunday. I volunteered to bring a lunch for us, and went to buy the groceries.

As I looked in the bread aisle I wondered if he'd prefer wheat, sourdough, pumpernickel or rye, so I bought a loaf of each. Then it was a decision among salami, ham, cheese, and turkey, so I bought some of each. Of course I bought mayonnaise and mustard, pickles (dill or sweet?), olives, and cookies. In the dorm kitchen I made an assortment of different meats with different breads in case he'd prefer ham on rye to ham on sourdough, etc. After I cut them in all in halves so he could have a variety from which to choose, I counted 32 sandwiches.

Pleased with my efforts, the next day I got into his car with the deli-in-a-bag to be opened at lunchtime. As I proudly rattled off 32 choices his expression turned from pleasure to puzzlement to annoyance.

"How many kinds did you make?" he queried, so I explained the process that had resulted in the number of options.

I was sobered at his disapproving dismay. He clearly thought me nuts. "What am I supposed to do with all these?" he asked.

"Well, you could take them back to your rooming house or to the radio station to share with the others."

"Just hand me any one of them," he ordered a bit sharply, and I continued trying to help him see the menu as evidence of my love and caring, but it didn't fly. We've laughed about it many times since.

two

You Mean We Have Differences?

Had we known then what we do now, we might have recognized a definite pattern. My goal in life was to please him with how much I adored him, and his goal was to avoid intimacy. I guess. I still can't quite get my head around anyone *not* liking intimacy, but he maintains it makes him uncomfortable.

To say it's been a challenge to us both for 60 years is a gross understatement. Many years ago I asked him, "What can I do for you to make you happy?"

His quick reply was, "Just leave me alone."

Shocked as I was, I knew his picture of the ideal relationship was vastly different from mine. But is either of us right or wrong? No! I know that now.

We have different preferences in interacting, is all. He belongs to every organization, group and committee in Tucson and Flagstaff. In fact if any of you start a new club about anything, he'd love to join! He delights in belonging to a group in which the members discuss how to solve problems. He sits among them, content to discuss any subject for hours and hours. But he gets antsy if feelings come into the discussion. That's getting dangerously close to intimacy, and non-glommers resist going there. They like discussions on religion, gas prices, brands of beer, people they know, locations all over the world, history, geography, iPads, space craft, movies, TV shows, books, car details and sports of all kinds.

Ask any non-glommers how they feel, though, and you see the deer-in-the-headlights expression of panic. Larry often says he's afraid he'll give the wrong answer.

I remind him there is *no* wrong answer. It's just describing a feeling, but by then he's out the kitchen door to… well, it doesn't matter where. Just as long as he's out of the room I'm in, torturing him with impossible questions.

Glommers, on the other hand, can happily discuss their emotions ad nauseam, and they have feelings about hundreds of different subjects, going back to tot-hood.

Communication

I'm happiest in one-on-one settings. Having lunch with a friend gives both of us a chance to learn how the other one feels about all manner of things.

Conversely, I can be content in a group and able to enjoy the conversation, but in my heart I'd so rather be talking to any one person of the group, intimately.

The best situation is one on one with another glommer who's sensitive to feelings and eager to share theirs and mine. To me, conversation is what life is all about.

Of course I believe that there is a lot of "conversation" delivered without words, and that's good or bad depending on the situation. I'm thinking of love exhibited between two people, in which a hug or a kiss and even just looking at one another's face is a beautiful way of getting a message across. Holding hands, a pat on the shoulder as one walks by the other, a smile: all transmit affection and make the recipient feel happier than a moment before.

I taught moms and dads in parenting classes that communication is 75% *non*-verbal, and a wonderful way to let your children know how much you love them and believe in them.

An example would be a child coming home from school as a parent is reading the paper. The child excitedly says, "Guess what! I got a part in the school play!"

Parent can respond in many ways or in a combination of techniques. First by putting the paper down and just looking at the child with joy. Even by not speaking at all, the parent is letting the child see the glow and pride in his or her face. Maybe then reaching out and drawing the child closer adds additional affection, and then using words emphasizes the message.

"Oh, I am so happy for you, sweetie! When did you find out?"

Give the child a moment to respond, and if there's no comment, the parent can continue with another question or statement.

"Do you know yet when the play will be? I can't wait to come and see you onstage! Let's call all your grandparents tonight, so you can tell them, too."

Let the child have plenty of time to talk, and when he's finished you can end with something like "Well, you just gave me the best news I could have had today." Don't pick the paper up until it's clear there's no more to say on either side.

The danger of using *only* your words is the incompleteness of the encounter. I might have continued looking at the paper as I said, "Wow, that's great!" But without the 75% body language the overall effect won't be nearly as nurturing to the child.

The same dynamics work every bit as well with one's spouse/lover.

Just for fun, let's look at the 32-sandwich picnic lunch from 60 years ago. Suppose, as I opened the big bag and began listing the choices, Larry had said, "How many kinds did you make? *No!! Really??* You took that much time and put so much thought into our menu today? I'm in awe of you!" For the loving body language he would pull over and stop the car, turn off the ignition and gaze at me in adoration.

Now I know all of you non-glommers are thinking, "Good grief, this dame would make me crazy! She expects me to say and do all that? Yeah, I like that she fixed some food, but she shouldn't have gone to all that trouble. It's not that big a deal."

Wouldn't life be simpler if we felt okay about putting something like this into Craigslist: "Glommer looking for another glommer. Non-glommers needn't apply."

Sadly, however, nobody would understand what it means. Actually, they might guess it's some form of sexual activity with which they're not yet familiar. In fact, I might be flooded with entries.

Next time you throw a party for your single friends, consider handing out blank stick-on cards as they arrive. During the pre-dinner drinks you explain the glom theory after which they fill in their identity. It would so interesting to see the proportion of both kinds, and then to watch the behavior. I suspect the different types would gather together to discuss the flaws of the other group. Of course many wouldn't dream of being so honest, but you're trying for scientific statistics.

People often suggest that more women are glommers than men, and I agree in part. But I know many male glommers, too; some married non-glommers and are sorry they made the wrong choice.

There is a definite wide line between glommers and controlling mates. A plain old ordinary glommer seeks to spend quality time with her partner but has no desire to run his life. She's not jealous of his friends, work, social activities, nothing, as long as she gets affection and good conversation with him, but that last phrase is the key to her intentions; the "as long as she gets affection and good conversation with him."

If she doesn't, she's sure to find herself jealous of all the activities in his life that he prefers to her company.

A controller does want to manage his life, and that's bound to push the partner away. We all resist control.

What Does Your Pie Chart Say?

A couple who came for marriage counseling years ago were struggling with the rules within. He was a definite controller, refusing to let his wife see even her obstetrician unless he was with them the whole time. Not only that, she wasn't allowed to talk to any neighbor man if she happened upon him at the mailbox. Nor could she have her brothers over to watch a movie with her if her husband was out with his friends.

Naturally she was feeling controlled and resenting it bitterly. I pointed out the concept of mutual respect: that any two people must treat each other with respect. You and I must respect one another, and we must also respect ourselves. If any of those areas of respect are missing, the relationship will probably fail eventually.

The husband disagreed angrily with me and wasn't willing to discuss it, so I haven't seen them since. Anyone want to bet they're not married anymore?

He was *not* a glommer. Perhaps we could find out what a glommer is by using a pie chart. The whole pie is 24 hours of time, and we get to choose how we'll spend that 24 hours.

Around a third of it is for sleep. Probably work takes up another third. Of the eight hours left there are many chores we face, like getting to work and back, which can take anywhere from 20 minutes to an hour or more. Doing housework, cooking, keeping up with the yard, with laundry, maybe parenting, attending meetings, a huge number of minor tasks that add up to several hours.

How much conversation time do you think is fair to ask of your lover?

A male artist said simply, "I want her to be my whole pie." She didn't want to be, and that marriage was soon to end.

You already know I'm a glommer, so I would delight in an hour a day of togetherness. Okay, so what's togetherness? Going to a movie? Not so much, because there's little conversation involved. Dinner out? *Yes!* There's lots of time to talk. Watching TV at home as long as you both talk during commercials and maybe before and after, too.

You already know Larry is a non-glommer, so he resists any activity that calls for conversation. Our pies might match pretty well for 18 to 22 hours as we go about daily living, but we vary enormously in our desire for conversation time. I'd be content with 20 minutes a day of eye-to-eye "soul sharing," telling and hearing each other's thoughts, hopes, dreams and fears; *not* just exchanging information about politics or the state of the world. I like those topics, too, but not instead of the intimate ones.

Often couples chat while they're doing some kind of work together, like gardening or painting a room. Cooking could lend itself to sharing thoughts and feelings, or walking the dog. The trouble is that some people find those experiences disagreeable, and their moods are dark and dismal. They don't enjoy the tasks, so they don't like to have pleasant conversations along with what they see as "tedious work."

Couples with similar interests, of course, are the luckiest. Our neighbors both love to camp out. He hunts while she walks and revels in being so close to nature. He bags a deer, and she skins and butchers it. It's terrific teamwork in which both share the same goals and enjoy every minute.

We have friends who love to golf and others whose life is filled with music; they play instruments and perform in programs together.

But on the other hand there are couples who haven't a single common interest except for enjoying their children. When the kids are grown and gone there's little to bond the parents. Neither enjoys participating in what the other loves.

They feel bad about it. They know they have no commonality, and neither wants to hurt the mate, but neither do they want to share experiences.

They probably have the most difficult time of all, but, again, neither one of them is right or wrong, good or bad. Generally they remain together because it's practical. Both like the family home and the fact that the kids can all come home and share holidays with them.

They genuinely *like* each other, so they make it work.

The Magic Geranium

Though the focus of this book is understanding glommers and non-glommers, we get a surprise bonus in the process, and that happens in many areas of life.

For instance, let's say I want to lose 20 pounds. I decide not only to change my eating habits but also to increase my exercise. Every day I eat more healthily and I walk increasingly longer on my treadmill. Sure enough, I find myself losing weight. Yay!

I keep up the meal plan I'm using *and* I can walk longer every week. To my delight, I feel better. I discover I have more energy and more enthusiasm as well. Those positive traits give me more confidence, and I find myself having more friends than I did before.

The process reminds me of a story our children enjoyed when they were small called "The Magic Geranium." It was about a woman who lived in an old, run-down house. One day in a grocery store she saw a small geranium plant which she bought and happily took home.

She set it on her kitchen table which had a shabby old cloth on it. Suddenly the table looked so run down she decided to paint it. Shortening the story considerably, she painted it white and then noticed how shabby the wall behind it had become.

Nothing would do but painting the wall a nice soft shade of apple green, but then the dirty window looked dirtier. She washed it and polished it till it sparkled, which showed its curtain to be dull and faded.

From her ragbag she found an old skirt that no longer fit her, but had enough fabric in it to stitch up a pair of curtains. Their bright red flowered print looked simply beautiful against the soft green wall!

Then she sat down and admired her kitchen. She was so thrilled to see the beauty everywhere, she folded her hands and beamed with joy. Then she said, "It's a beautiful kitchen now, and all because of that magic geranium!"

While the story details are dim in my memory, I felt glad all over each time I read the book, and I realized way back then that we human beings are like that kitchen.

We become figuratively dusty and faded, old and tired-looking, dull and dismal, bored and boring. We may become discouraged and depressed and even despairing.

But one day we might notice an announcement in the paper inviting us to a free presentation of a musical program or an art exhibit. We decide to go see it, so we clean ourselves up a bit and off we go.

It inspires us, and we feel a surge of excitement as we walk back home, remembering an old box of paints in a closet. Of course we hurry home, get out the paints and paint a picture that we like so much, it opens a door to a new and wonderful hobby.

We know the paints are not magic, nor was the exhibit, but somewhere there we got excited about a change in our lives.

All we need is one bit of inspiration that ignites our pilot light and begins a spiral of new insights and options we can use for any problem.

So if you're a glommer or a non-glommer who's less than happy, this process can change your life. Likewise, if you're miserable in your job, you might find some helpful resources in this book.

If your family life is not very rewarding (or maybe it absolutely stinks), the one behavior you choose to change can become your magic geranium.

The single point I'll keep making in as many ways as I can is this: We cannot ever change any else's behavior. At least not any adult's. They can change their own behavior, but only if they choose to. But we have *ever* so much power over our own behavior.

We may not often see it, and even when we do, we may choose not to use it, but it's always there for us.

I like the teeter-totter comparison. If you and I are on opposite ends of a teeter-totter we cooperate and combine our power to keep it going up and down. Should either of us get tired of the game, we might just jump off, rendering the partner no longer able to continue the movement.

So the following pages are suggestions for you. Use them to find solutions to any issue you may have with anyone. Know that even when you find some dandy solutions, you may decide not to use them, and that's your privilege. We may get more pleasure out of hating someone than we would by changing jobs.

Knowing that could be helpful to you in understanding why you stay in a place which makes you miserable. You're probably getting some kind of pay-off, and you might choose to hang onto it for the rest of your life. If you do, try to enjoy it, at least!

What Makes You Happy?

When I was in my mid-twenties Larry and I were head residents in a men's dorm at Northern Arizona University. Of the hundred and sixty boys who lived there, I remember a dozen or so for special reasons. One because he was such a troublemaker, one because he made us laugh all the time, one who played the bongos long into the night. Another who baby-sat for us, one who ran through a huge plate glass window, and one whom I had a secret crush on.

And then there was Robert the cynic. He was a handsome young man who rode a motorcycle and always looked grim. One day he asked us if we'd be willing to save him the weather report from our daily newspaper, because it would be helpful in his science class. Each afternoon he'd knock on our door and we'd hand him the column, and now and then he'd come in and talk for a few minutes.

He was the first source from which I heard, "You never do anything unless you get a reward from it."

"Robert, I totally disagree," I said. "I do lots of things that I don't enjoy doing; things that in no way give me anything positive."

"Name one," he challenged.

"Saving you the weather column," I answered smugly. "It's a bit of a nuisance cutting it out every day, but I do it anyway as a favor to you."

"And that makes you feel good," he countered. "You know it helps me and I appreciate it, and that's your payoff. You wouldn't do it for any other reason—nobody would."

We continued to argue that point for a few weeks until both became convinced the other would never reverse opinions, and finally we dropped it. His science class ended and Robert quit calling. Sometimes I wonder what became of him, because I'd like to tell him now that I've changed my mind; I think he's right.

Pursuing pleasure is an important motivator in everyone's life, and yet it can be difficult to recognize. Some of our behavior appears to be totally altruistic, unselfish and totally lacking in any kind of obvious fun, and yet there is some payoff in it or we wouldn't do it. (Robert, wherever you are, I can't believe I'm saying those words.)

Often the tasks we do might even be odious ones, jobs we absolutely hate, and yet we do them. We want whatever that reward is. It might be the paycheck we receive every two weeks, or the pat on the back from someone who appreciates our efforts. It could be seeing results. A body builder who grunts in pain as he hefts those weights gets to see and feel his muscles becoming big and tough. A musician who practices for long, tiresome hours can hear the results as weeks go by.

A husband who nurses his wife through months of a fatal illness feels enormous satisfaction in knowing he's helping her the best he can. A parent choking back tears as Junior goes off to the Navy feels sadness but also gladness at watching him do what he's chosen to do.

Of course the obvious pleasures motivate us: eating and drinking, pursuing our interests, enjoying relationships, the things we can easily see that make life fun for us. But there are so very many unrecognized goals and payoffs behind every action we do, and some of them are downright uncomfortable.

Have you ever "cut off your nose to spite your face?" My teenage friend Kate longs to play the guitar, and her mother, who is a musician, keeps urging her to get one and take lessons. Unfortunately Kate gets more pleasure out of defeating her mother than she would from enjoying a guitar. So depriving herself of that experience gives her more compensation than playing music would. Most of us can relate to that kind of thinking somewhere in our lives, past or present.

We who watch our weight and our health probably avoid certain foods that we sometimes crave, and it's easy to feel sorry for ourselves. We're fulfilling a greater goal, though, by choosing long-term satisfaction over immediate gratification.

There is one more motivator that speaks to us all, however, and it's a big one. It is avoiding pain. Though it sounds simplistic, I believe the two forces that most control our lives are pursuing pleasure and avoiding pain. Of the two, avoiding pain is the stronger influence, and most of us will do almost anything to honor that one.

Pain, of course, is in the head of the person's feeling it, and what is painful to me might not be a bit painful to you. I just had lunch with my friend Virginia, and I wore nice comfortable flat sandals. She was wearing four-inch heels that made me wince just seeing them. "Oh, you poor thing, don't your feet hurt?" I asked sympathetically.

She looked at me strangely and said, "Why would they hurt?"

"Those high heels!"

"I love to wear heels," she insisted. "I even put them on to go grocery shopping. I feel better in them than I do in little dinky heels."

High heels represent pain to me, so I avoid them whenever possible. To Virginia they represent pleasure, which she seeks. The fact that something so simple and ordinary can symbolize opposite extremes to two people demonstrates the difficulty we have understanding larger issues and their ramifications. Each of us has all kinds of pains and pleasures we're trying to seek or avoid, and much of the time we're unaware of how personal the definitions are.

A particular activity might bring tremendous pleasure to one group of people and only pain to another group. In the years that Larry and I were head residents at NAU we often laughed that we had to stick together up there because we were the misfits. It seemed like the entire faculty and staff of the college played bridge. They were very friendly in inviting us to bridge parties, which obviously brought them a great deal of pleasure. To Larry and me bridge was boring and a source of pain, so we found other things to do.

How can so many things evoke opposite responses in so many people? We're all just wired differently, that's all, and no one can say these people are right and those are wrong. Like some of us have A-positive blood and some O-negative, we all have our own preferences.

Those preferences make up our individual lists of values. And if we asked a thousand people to write down on lists all the pleasures they'd like to pursue and all the pain they're trying to avoid, we'd have a thousand variations. My hunch is that no two would match.

Come to think of it, those lists would really simplify life, wouldn't they? Perhaps we should all write out our lists and have a hundred copies made. Then every time we met someone new we could exchange lists right off the bat, scan them quickly, and know how much or how little we have in common. It would cut through hours and hours of conversation as we try to get to know one another. But I guess it wouldn't be nearly as much fun as getting to know someone in depth, so let's junk that idea.

Still, it might be helpful to us as individuals to make those lists for our own self-understanding, particularly when we find ourselves having difficulty achieving something we're working toward. Sometimes we work like Trojans trying to change a trait or habit. We make some progress and then slip back into our old ways. Over and over and over we do that, building discouragement with every setback, feeling like we're weak, stupid ninnies because we've not been able to change.

It would be very helpful to realize the stumbling block that keeps getting in our way, and usually that's the pain-pleasure principle. Most of us are likely to go to great lengths to avoid what seems too painful to confront.

One of the biggies is others' disapproval. It takes a whopping amount of self-esteem to be able to hear criticism and not feel discomfited by it.

Certainly that's the kind of person I hope to become eventually. My dream is getting to the point at which I can listen to someone lay into me full blast, cussing me out, raking me over the coals, shouting what a failure I am, what a stupid, miserable excuse for a human being, etc. etc., and feel absolutely no pain. When that day comes I'll be able to hear those comments with some interest but no discomfort. I'll be thinking, "Isn't it interesting that's how that person sees me. Fancy that!" with nary a flicker of hurt or anger. I'll feel exactly the same as I do watching a movie: interested, perhaps even fascinated, but not applying it to myself. I know I'm worthwhile, so I won't fall into my old pattern of feeling stabbed when someone sees me as unworthy.

Like I say, that's my dream. I'm a pretty long way from reaching that goal, and so far I feel hurt when I'm verbally attacked, but I am absolutely sure it's possible to attain that attitude. One of the best ways to reach any goal is to practice it. So I can use my desire to achieve that wondrous state as a means of gaining pleasure, feeling pleased whenever I get the opportunity for some practice.

That would reverse my belief that I must avoid others' disapproval, knowing I can use their disapproval in order to gain pleasure. It would mean "changing the channel" as I do when watching TV, only the channels are in my head.

When there's a show I find dull or unsatisfactory for any reason I can continue watching it and feeling bored and dissatisfied, or I can change the channel to something I'll enjoy. We have that same ability inside our heads. We can decide to focus on any subject we wish, on any attitude or belief that appeals to us. We're never "stuck" on one thought process unless we choose to stay there, and yet you'd think we were. So often we dwell on a negative picture or thought for hours and even days, hating it and yet not realizing we have the power to change it.

How freeing it is to become aware we can find a different "movie," thought or picture. Once we know we can do that, we get to decide if we will, and that's often harder than it sounds.

One would think we'd never deliberately watch a show that makes us miserable in preference to one we'd find entertaining, but we do. Figuring out why gives us a clue to our payoff—a very important step in changing.

Let's say one of my lifelong claims to fame is being "sweet." If I've gotten praise and recognition for that characteristic all these years, it's become a source of pleasure for me.

So far so good, nothing wrong with that.

Okay, but say a friend has gotten into a habit that's driving me crazy. Maybe he taps his fingers on the table incessantly, absentmindedly, and it gets on my nerves something fierce.

Now I have a problem. I want to seek pleasure by continuing my image of being The Sweet One, so I'm reluctant to tell him how annoyed I've gotten at his finger tapping. On the other hand I want to avoid pain by ridding the atmosphere of bothersome noises. How can I possibly solve this problem? So far I've said nothing, maintaining a calm, placid expression, while inside I'm becoming a seething mass of resentment. I'm getting hostile with this jerk not only for disturbing the peace but also for putting me in a position in which I might have to abandon "sweet" or lose my sanity.

Those are the typical tensions our every day lives are fraught with: not big, earthshaking crises, but incidents that threaten our peace of mind.

If I want a solution I need to make the negative action into one that's positive to me. What a golden opportunity to make myself grow! This is my own private "lab" in which I can experiment with my behavior and run tests and see what happens. If I really want to achieve the state of bliss I described before, being unfazed by criticism and disapproval, here's my chance to practice.

Wonder of wonders, if I have the courage to do it, it might resolve two issues at the same time. All I need to do is see the positive, the pleasure, in asserting myself—even knowing it might bring disapproval. If it does I get to practice allowing that to happen and feeling myself grow stronger in surviving it. Would having the courage to risk disapproval bring me pleasure? You bet!

Terrific. And it might even stop the finger tapping, although there are no guarantees about that. At the very least, though, it will be the first step in finding a resolution or compromise about finger tapping. And the biggest plus will be my willingness to take on a very growth-producing behavior and see what happens.

three

Making the Choice

So now I can pursue pleasure and avoid pain at the same time. Of course there's still some pain or discomfort in carrying out the exercise, but that's true with any exercise. Remember the body builder? Once my reasons are clear and my goals are defined it's much easier to put up with the discomfort, knowing it will bring me closer to my goal.

Just as cleaning the bathroom (pain) is bearable because of a greater purpose (the pleasure of a sparkling bathroom), I can now do something about my finger-happy friend. I'm no longer stuck. I'm not helpless or powerless anymore. Once we take back our power we're halfway there.

I might also be pondering the wisdom of keeping The Sweet One as my image. Is it truly bringing me enough pleasure to warrant all the pain I have to endure in that role? Maybe I'd like to change that title to The Brave One. Would acting courageously make me feel good about myself?

Again, I can change channels. If you have a remote control for your TV set you can sit comfortably on your couch and "look at the menu." You may be one who loves to flip from channel to channel just to check out all the possibilities before you settle down to one show. Or you might read the paper or TV Guide to discover what's available before you even turn on the set.

You can do the same with your mind. As the star of your own show you get to be whatever image you feel like being. If being The Sweet One is filling your needs, then don't change it. I never argue with success. But know that you can change it any time your heart desires; that's the most important knowledge. You can be The Brave One, or The Happy One, The Leader, The Mellow One, The Romantic One, The Cut-Up, and furthermore you can be all of those or any of those, anytime you please!

Nowhere is it written that we must be one type of person and only one type forevermore. We get to incorporate every personality type we can think of in our own behavior, and we can change ourselves at the slightest whim.

One of the worst habits we can pick up is that of defining ourselves as "the kind of person who…" When we do that we keep ourselves stuck in a pigeonhole that imprisons us. Granted, it may also keep us safe by maintaining the status quo. That's appealing to some people. It also serves to excuse our holding onto bad behavior, which may be a form of manipulation.

"I'm the kind of person who never forgives" is a clear message to those around us that they'd better be careful never to cross us.

"I'm the kind of person who yells and screams and gets it all out, and then I forget it" implies that "I have permission to act as disrespectfully as I want, and then we'll all forget my bad behavior."

"I'm the kind of person who worries, so I need my family to tell me where they are at all times" is a way of saying, "Since I am a worrier, I have the right to insist on knowing your business."

Frequently categorizing ourselves serves several purposes at once, and we're understandably reluctant to change that behavior. We will change only if we're convinced it will make us happier.

So, again, if you're already happy with your life, don't rock the boat. In fact, go write your own self-help book and I'll buy one, because I'm always looking for ways to become still happier!

When a new show comes onto the television networks most of us give it at least a quick perusal to see if we might enjoy it. If not, we never have to watch it again. I suggest we do the same with the shows in our heads. If I am The Sweet One much of the time, it would be fun to try being The Brave One and see if I like it. I'm not required to stay there. I can imagine how it feels to be brave, and I can guess what brave people do. I can think of brave characters in books and movies and watch how they respond to situations that I face in my own life.

Then I can "act as if." I get to try my hand as an actress and play like I am a brave one, even though I know I'm new at that role. It just happens to be a role I've never played before, but it doesn't mean I'm not equipped to play it.

My original family was not very physical. There wasn't much touching or hugging or kissing, though there was warmth and affection and certainly respect. You might guess, and you'd be correct, that I grew up a non-toucher, and I was content with that for a long time. When I went back to school at forty I found the people in the counseling and guidance department were very touchy. There were hugs galore, and just simple pats on the arm or the shoulder, and I liked that. But I was aware that I was "the kind of person" who didn't touch.

I admired the physical folks, however, enough that I determined to act as if I were touchy, too. At first it was uncomfortable. It felt strained and unnatural to me to reach out and make contact with a friend. It seemed phony and wooden, and I half expected everyone to laugh at my clumsy efforts. In fact nobody seemed to notice one way or another. And I was getting a kick out of pretending I was a toucher, so I kept doing it.

"Fake it till you make it," people say, and it works. Now I'm just as good at hugging as anybody in the whole world. It was a matter of changing the channel in my mind, making the star in my movie a toucher instead of a constrained person.

What a feeling of power we enjoy when we've learned a new behavior! Frequently we're inspired to learn something else once we know we can.

Children are so eager to learn and try new behavior that they learn huge amounts of information and skills by the time they're ready for school. Little by little, though, we become inhibited, and too often we become afraid of trying out new behavior.

Usually, by the time we're adults we've defined ourselves so precisely that we live by those definitions, excluding all the millions of descriptions that are still available to us. It takes some courage to be willing to add new facets to our personalities, but if we can see value in doing it we just might.

The whole process is simply weighing and deciding: what's the pain I'm trying to avoid? How can I make that pleasurable? Am I willing to try it out? Try it on? Act as if? Fake it? What the heck, why not!

Getting to decide how we're going to act is one of the most precious freedoms we have in this world, and most of the time we're not much aware of it. In fact, I tend to say, "I have to…" way more than "I get to."

In an awareness group I attended years ago, the leader asked us to make a list of all the things we had to do the day before. We wrote long lists, most of us starting with "I had to get up."

She pointed out then that we didn't really have to get up if we didn't want to. We could have stayed in bed till we rotted. Naturally we'd lose our jobs and eventually our lives as we starved to death there under the covers, but getting up was something we didn't have to do. We chose to do it. We didn't have to shower or get dressed. We would have been arrested if we'd walked down the street naked, but it was our choice. Our co-workers would avoid us if we stank, but no one could force us to take showers.

We caught on pretty quickly and realized there wasn't much we really had to do after all; most of our behavior was chosen as the best of the available options. Then we changed our lists all the way down the page, replacing "I have to" with "I choose to." It was a good little lesson of awareness; one I haven't forgotten. I still say, "I have to stop and get gas," and a hundred other things like that, but if I think about it I know I don't have to get gas. I have the right to run out of gas if I prefer.

I like to take that a step further and replace "have" or "choose" with "get." I get to get up in the morning. And all day long I get to do the things that enhance my life, even though many of them are nuisance things. Like getting gas. It certainly became a precious experience when there was a gas shortage years ago, and we all waited in long lines at the gas pumps. The minute gas was easily available, however, it became a have-to again.

One of my goals is becoming more aware of all the get-to's in my life. I think if I consciously realized them, I'd be so much more appreciative of everything.

It rarely occurs to us how nice it is being able to swallow—not until we have sore throats. Most of us don't sit around at coffee breaks, beaming at one another and saying, "Isn't it fun to swallow?" Even if we thought it we probably wouldn't share that awareness, and that may be just as well.

But I believe my consciousness of how nice it is to swallow would add to my overall happiness level. If I were cognizant of even a fraction of the get-to's in my day, I'd be ecstatic most of the time. I get to pick out what clothes I want to put on. I get to decide what to eat for breakfast. I get to eat! (That's one of life's greatest joys.) I get to feel energetic enough to neaten the house, to throw a load of clothes in the washer and dryer, and to read the paper—another hugely satisfying occupation. Then I get to work with people, helping them solve their problems, and so on—all day long. In the evening, after I've gotten to decide what to fix for dinner and enjoyed it, I get to watch my favorite TV programs and finally to settle into the bed I actively adore. What a life!

When I stop and think about it I know I have very little to complain about, but the fact is I don't stop and think about it often. And worse, I am usually in a snit about some triviality or other. The olive oil spot on the carpet that even the pros can't get out. The creak in my car that defies the mechanics. The five pounds that insist on clinging to my body in spite of my loathing of them. ("I get to eat!") And so on, ad nauseam.

The level of happiness I feel is in direct proportion to the number of get-to's I entertain, and I sabotage that when I choose to focus on the olive oil spot. It's definitely my choice.

Most likely we would all prefer to look more at the get-to's and less at the annoyances of life. Then why is it so hard to do? We can read a book like this, nod with recognition, decide to focus on the positive hereafter, and in about five seconds be dwelling on the negative again. I do it all the time. How can we stay on the positive track?

One suggestion is to go to an office supply store and buy a box of little bitty stick-on dots. They come in many colors and sizes and you get to choose one. Or two or three! Then you peel them off and stick them to objects you see often in your everyday life.

Put one on the bathroom mirror and one on the toilet flusher. Every time you see one you think, "I get to…" and provide the logical word. In this case it could be "I get to see how good looking I am," or "…enjoy the fresh taste of my toothpaste," or whatever the cabinet mirror means to you. As you flush you might say, "I get to enjoy the feeling of relief!" or "…be glad I eat so much fiber," or "…weigh less than I did a minute ago." Whatever.

You stick the little dots on your hair dryer ("I get to have instant access to instruments that make me gorgeous") and on your coffee maker ("I get to make coffee precisely as strong as I like it"). Maybe one could go on your refrigerator, the marmalade jar, the toaster, the dishwasher, etc.

How about one on your key chain? That represents a wealth of blessings in your life. Your steering wheel? And your workplace might offer dozens of objects that you get to use in making your living.

You get the idea. No, the copy machine is not generally looked at as a fun toy, and yet it does simplify your life tremendously. You get to make copies mechanically instead of having to handle carbon paper. The phone saves you countless hours of typing letters.

At home your vacuum cleaner makes cleaning a lot simpler than using the old carpet sweeper. Those little bright dots serve to make us aware, maybe for the first time, how many things do enhance our lives. And the process changes our thinking from the grim, "I have to clean the sink" to "I get to make the sink gleam."

Does it sound too Pollyanna-ish for your taste? Okay, I have to admit I haven't actually done it, either.

But I may one day. I like to think I would for sure if I were depressed or out of sorts for more than a day or so. You don't need gimmicks if you're already pretty aware of how good life is to you, but if you feel you lean toward the pessimistic side you can give it a try. It's a no-fail recipe for brightening your outlook, for as long as you want to leave the little dots up.

Sooner or later you'd get so used to them you wouldn't notice them anymore, so you'd peel them off. Maybe you'd like to stick different ones up as reminders of some kind. Like jogging your memory to stand up straight or hold in your tummy or tell some family member you appreciate him or her.

In a way it's rearranging your outlook, putting the positive ahead of the negative. Actually life is an endless process of rearranging, it seems to me. From our birth, when we get removed from Mom's womb, to death, when we move from earth to heaven, we're simply being rearranged. And the whole time in between we are rearranging things. The food from our plates into our mouths. The toys out of the toy box and back in again. Clothes from the closet onto our bodies. Shoes from the shoe store into our closets. We're constantly putting things away, neatening our houses and our desks. Papers into the trash, books from the library to our cars, our bedrooms, and back to the library. We rearrange our furniture and even our places of residence as we change addresses.

Hopefully we do the same thing inside our heads: rearrange our thoughts and our priorities. Different issues come into focus and take first place in our thinking. With new information and awareness we throw away old, stale beliefs and replace them with fresh enthusiasm and challenging concerns.

That doesn't mean we won't rearrange them back where they were as we go along. We may see we were right in the first place. But let's enjoy the continuing process. We get to love it or hate it. Loving's more fun.

The Three-Legged Stool

Experts tell us that the most balanced people among us are like three-legged stools, each leg having an important role in making our lives work smoothly.

The first leg is SELF-PRESERVATION. We all are born with a need to take care of ourselves by eating, drinking, having a home in which to live, seeing doctors if we need their help, being safe from freezing or blistering weather, etc. We innately know what we need, and we hope to make sure we can fill those needs.

(I just used the word "need" incorrectly. Our real needs are simply food, water, and shelter. All the other things we desire are "wants," no matter how strongly we desire them. However we generally refer to them as "needs," so I'm using that word.)

The second leg is BELONGING TO SOCIETY. Most of find jobs that help society in some way, and we interact with many people in the course of working and of communicating for many reasons. Some of it may be strictly for enjoyment, which is highly valuable to us. Little kids begin their lives learning to play with other little kids; they learn how to accept each other, how to protect and how to share. That's where the mutual respect gets most of its workout, discovering the rules of fairness.

The third leg is LOVE & INTIMACY. Instinctively we find the members of the opposite gender becoming interesting to us in the teen years, if not before. (Those born with homosexual DNA will, of course, be attracted to people of their same sex.) Either way, we find ourselves desiring intimacy. Nature supplies with us goodly amounts of desire, in fact, to make sure we keep reproducing.

Those three legs keep the stool in balance, but most of us find our legs are of different lengths. While it might simplify life if all the legs were the same size, it's not usually the case.

You can tell the length of each of your legs by picturing yourself at a party. Upon entering I move around the room greeting all the people I see (Belonging To Society), but very soon I'm taking care of my most important leg (Self-Preservation).

I seek out a glass of wine and scope out the food table to see what looks good to eat a little later on. All the while I'm looking for a friend with whom I can chat comfortably and lengthily. When I find her or him I say, "Can we sit a bit?" and head for a two-person spot.

That's when the party becomes delightful, as I'm sipping wine and talking with someone who wants to talk as much as I do. I would be happy sitting in that very chair, enjoying this one-on-one chat for the rest of the evening.

Well, not quite, because my tummy begins to sound hungry, and I suggest we get a bite to eat. Ideally we get plates of tasty foods and return to our conversation. Now the party truly *is* perfect.

I've no idea where Larry is, because he's busily moving from guest to guest having relatively short conversations with each. He seldom eats, preferring not to interrupt talking with as many people as he can.

Our three legs show clearly as we discuss the party on the way home. "Wasn't that a great party?" I might begin. "I *loved* the food, and I got to have a long talk with Marty. We sat on the sofa near the fireplace and got caught up."

You notice my Self-Preservation was provided by the food, the wine, and the comfortable sofa. The desire for intimacy was met by my long discussion with Marty.

But what about the Social leg? Oh, I did politely greet and share a few words with the hosts and most of the guests, but that was incidental. My need for Socialness is really quite small.

My Self-Preservation leg seems to tie with the Intimacy leg. And the Social leg is hardly there at all.

Larry has virtually no need for Self-Preservation or Intimacy, but a huge intense desire for Sociability. He would spend the evening exchanging information with dozens of people, having no need to talk about feelings or anything intimate. Those he'd avoid like the plague.

So both of us would have enjoyed the party, but from two entirely different points of view.

Thus is our life. Neither of us is much interested in the other's most important need.

You can enjoy figuring out the size of your three legs by picturing a party you'd attend, and how you'd spend your time and energy.

While it might be ideal if a couple had matching three-legged desires, it isn't essential. We learn to understand each other's preferences and accept them.

What *doesn't* work is trying to change the other's preferences. "You spent the whole time talking to Marty. Why didn't you mingle more?" "You didn't eat? How could you skip all that delicious food? You should have at least had something protein-y."

Sometimes a party will thrill one person and leave the other totally cold, like a table with only chips and dips and beer. Plus a group of strangers all talking about their jobs. I'd walk away from that declaring it the worst party ever. Larry'd have a grand time.

But put us in a small group of foodies all of whom happen to be intimacy seekers who love to hear one another's feelings about almost anything, and it would be my pinnacle of joy. Larry would endure the situation politely but be eager to leave as soon as possible.

Is either of us right or wrong? Not a bit.

Some of us are not able to utilize all three legs. A Catholic priest or nun, for instance, is not supposed to have physical intimacy with anyone, though conversational intimacy might be allowed.

Many married couples just stop having sex somewhere along the way, though often one or the other continues to hunger for sex. That becomes a difficulty for both if they meant to honor their marriage vows. They're stuck between a rock and a hard place.

They can divorce, certainly, and many do, but that opens another can of worms as they deal with custody of children and a lot of hurt feelings all around.

They can stay married and cheat on their spouses, also generally a source of guilt and pain. They can stay married and live celibate lives, also a non-satisfying solution that can cause more pain than pleasure.

Both parties generally find themselves resenting their partners much of the time, blaming them for their unhappiness.

Sometimes a good marriage counselor can help them find the source of the loss of desire, but often neither person is willing to make the changes that would result in a happy sex life again. Or if even one of the persons is willing to change, it won't help unless both dedicate themselves to life changes that would improve the relationship.

The glommer will say, "I *want* intimacy, but I want it across the board. If we talk with each other and show some affection, it's easy and comfortable to turn the affection into sex. But after a day of distancing I can't go to bed and be able to turn suddenly sexual."

The non-glommer will say, "You know I love you. I married you, didn't I? I can't figure out why you don't want sex. I don't have anything to talk about, but sex is how I show my love."

Again neither party is "the bad guy." The chemistry simply isn't working, and the couple would both have to want to repair it in order to find sex natural and satisfying again.

When any of the three legs on the stool is not functioning, the owner of that leg must find an outlet to take its place.

Say one is receiving chemo for cancer and literally fighting for one's life. S/he is focused almost entirely on Self-Preservation, and may not have any interest in either Society or Intimacy. The partner will have to put more effort into his or her own society and/or intimacy in order to keep the stool on its feet… or foot. They hope that when the cancer is cured all three legs will be able to function well again.

The care of the three legs is virtually always shifting according to what else is happening in our lives. If one party is out of town on business the other will give more energy to Society and Self-Preservation. So will the out-of-town partner. Both know it's a temporary nuisance that will run its course and allow togetherness and intimacy to take its place once again.

Sadly, nobody is even the slightest bit aware of the three-legged stool when we're young and falling in love. Wouldn't it be wonderful if the subject were taught in high school? Young men and woman alike would be asking one another, "So what are your priorities in the three-legged stool? Oh, you're not into intimacy? Yeah, well, see you around."

When one leg is unable to be used we must put extra energy on the other two. Back to priests and nuns. With the intimacy leg blocked, they must turn their energies to the other two legs: Self-Preservation, since we all need to take care of ourselves, and Society, which would be crying out for their attention.

That's their profession: helping people. They must get a great deal of pleasure and satisfaction from doing that for most of their waking hours, but they, too, need a recreational kind of social contact.

We've gotten to be good friends with many of the priests who've lived at our church and have had them at our dinner parties many times. Most of them relish good food and enjoy a few drinks. Many have large stores of good jokes, and lots like to sing around the piano.

Back when color TV was new, Father O'Connor mentioned they'd just bought one. The other guests voiced some envy, since the rest of us still had black and white. He said with a grin, "You have your better halves; we have our better quarters." As well they should.

Sad are those who have *two* non-functioning legs. Let's look at a nun who needs to be isolated in a laboratory for some reason. Her Intimacy and her Social sides are both missing. She must put all her energy into Self-Preservation: caring for herself physically and also pampering herself in every way she can. Reading, watching TV, ideally having Netflix available, and listening to music.

Clearly it's a real challenge to find activities to replace the ones we'd like to be enjoying if we were able.

Taking it a step further, suppose you have all three legs missing. You're in a foreign prison, deprived of the ability to take care of yourself. You have nobody to talk to, and certainly no intimacy. You would indeed have a heck of a time enduring your situation. For me, prayer would be the only opportunity that might provide a bit of comfort in that extraordinary environment, and if you were a non-believer you'd be tremendously challenged in saving your sanity.

So we are lucky, we with three legs to work with. Our job is just to try to keep those operating as fully as we can. Those of us who have three functioning legs of priorities must try to keep them, and if one or more are hurting, we must tend to them as soon as possible and get them back in the groove.

Which is a good way of examining exactly what *is* the cause of our unhappiness.

As I said before, if we are married and are unhappy, our first belief is "I must have an unhappy marriage." Many times the marriage is not to blame; it's something else in our belief system that doesn't match our partner's belief system.

Ah *ha*, maybe the glommer/non-glommer factor?

That's an extremely common situation. A friend with whom I was having lunch recently asked what I'd been doing, and I told him about this book. He was fascinated and quickly offered, "I'm a glommer, and I'm married to a non-glommer. She probably should have stayed single."

And she probably should have, or married a non-glommer, for both their sakes. However, in that state of having fallen in love, we convince ourselves that everything will work absolutely splendidly!

I often suspect God engulfs us in that cloud of ecstasy so we'll marry and produce children to keep the world going. He probably also figures that being married will be good for us as far as learning to get along with someone with an entirely different set of beliefs and expectations. He is so right! There is no harsher education than marriage to teach us that we can't have our own way much of the time.

By the time we get to Heaven we will be polished and sanded down to perfection—humble, resilient, adaptable, confident and lovable. By then we'll all be the cream of the crop, and it's no wonder Heaven will be such a delight. Everybody will have been honed down to perfection before we even arrive there. I often say, "God sure knows what he's doing."

Since we didn't know all this when falling in love, what do we do with a challenged relationship *now*?

Often we've spent months or years trying one solution after another, often the very same methods. We try one, and if it doesn't work we try the same thing over again. And still again, ad nauseam. And we find ourselves still suffering with The Problem.

Truth be told, we probably hurt even more because frequently the solution becomes another problem! And we continue trying *that* solution over and over, so we're not only smarting over the original problem but now, additionally, with the new one.

Let me tell you about something that presented some wonderful insight into one of the ways we try to solve problems but actually make them worse.

four

Cages

I saw the small wrought-iron cage on a desk in my professor's office. Sitting on a bench inside the cage was a wrought-iron figure of a person—it could have been a man or a woman—holding onto the bars as he or she looked out longingly. There was an expression of resignation in the person's posture, and the message it conveyed was one of sad defeat and hopelessness.

Then I noticed that there was a door on the opposite side of the cage, and it was wide open.

I smiled when I saw it and felt impressed with the craftsperson who designed it—someone who saw a very common human experience and could create it in a tangible way.

"All the person has to do is stand up and walk out the door," I thought, "but he doesn't know it's open." And then as I looked at it, it occurred to me that he might know very well that there was a way out, but he preferred the cage to whatever was on the outside.

That was over forty years ago, and I've thought of the little cage from time to time when I see someone in an uncomfortable situation. Oftentimes "that person" has been myself.

Like most people, I have cages I can occupy at any time. Most of those cages, I created years ago when I was completely unaware of the process.

We always begin our cages as a means of taking care of ourselves, generally just stumbling onto the technique accidentally. At the time they serve a very important need in us and we deserve to be proud that we found a solution to our problem.

I heard a pediatrician tell a group of parents who were concerned at their children's thumb-sucking habit that they should feel pride in their babies for discovering their thumbs.

"Your bright little child has found a way to fill his need for comfort and nurturing," he explained. "You can enjoy feeling delighted in his independence at such a tender age."

It was an explanation that gladdened the hearts of all the parents, who from then on could stop worrying. But just as thumb-sucking can become a problem eventually, our well-intentioned remedies frequently create new difficulties.

So often the solution becomes a problem, and sometimes it takes us a long time to realize we now have to find a solution to that problem. But we mustn't blame ourselves, because the original discomfort we felt a long time ago was no doubt alleviated when we hit upon that solution. Like the baby feeling frustrated, we were delighted when our thumbs found our mouths and brought us solace. "Ah, there now," we thought, "that makes it all better."

Our present-day patterns of caring for ourselves are frequently as outdated as our thumb-sucking, but we've had them for so long that it often doesn't occur to us to change them. They've become "The Way One Does Things." As though chiseled in stone, they're habits we revere, and the very thought of abandoning them may incite panic in us.

By then they have become our cages and though we might hate them, we can't imagine life without them. "Give up my thumb? You've gotta be kidding." Except now it's "Give up my chocolate?" Or alcohol? Cigarettes, caffeine, sleeping pills—all can qualify as cages. So can relationships, and those may be the worst cages of all.

Relationships of any kind usually begin as positive experiences. We meet someone who becomes a friend. Often that's where the affiliation remains, for a short time or forever. Still, no matter what the duration, the friendship can become a cage to one or both parties.

Most of us have had acquaintances who complain about this friend or that. We had a neighbor who spent most of her time with her friend Alison and the rest of her time badmouthing Alison to the all the other neighbors.

"When we first moved into our house," the neighbor would say, "Alison came over with some home baked cookies, and she was so friendly we all just loved her. I was so glad to have a new friend, and we did everything together. She'd come over for coffee every morning, we'd shop, we'd take our kids swimming and we'd have picnics to get our families together.

"After a while I began to feel squeezed by her, like I couldn't do anything by myself—she constantly included herself in all my plans. I realized I had no other friends because I hadn't reached out to anyone else, since Alison was always handy.

"I never would have thought I'd come to resent her, but I do. I dread seeing her at my door every morning, and I have to make up excuses why I can't do everything with her anymore. I feel terrible about the whole thing, because I see the pain in her face when I refuse to go shopping, for instance.

"I feel smothered. She seems so dependent on me, and I want to back away and say, 'Look, get a life. I want to be with other people too.' How did I ever get into this mess? How can I get out of it without hurting Alison?"

I doubt she can. It sounds like Alison has become her cage, or one of her cages, for of course we can have many at one time.

When we find ourselves in an uncomfortable situation like that, we need to look at the theory of mutual respect I mentioned earlier: I must respect you. And you must respect me. In addition, you must respect yourself and I must respect myself. If all of those factors are balanced we have a dandy arrangement, but if any is out of kilter we feel uncomfortable.

Our discomfort is a symptom that might suggest an imbalance on the mutual respect scale, and once we realize that's what's causing our tension we know what we have to do. Well, we don't have to do anything if we prefer to continue suffering. But otherwise we need to correct the imbalance of respect.

Our neighbor was respecting Alison's needs but not her own. Alison was also respecting Alison's needs. Neighbor had to conjure up the courage to be honest, which is almost invariably the first step to solving our disrespect problems. She had to tell Alison what she was feeling even if it caused some discomfort on both sides. I would have said something like this:

"Alison, you have been such a close friend that I'm reluctant to say this because I'm afraid you'll be hurt. But if I don't say it I know I'm going to become resentful and eventually that will really destroy our friendship.

"I'm feeling restless for additional friends in my life. I don't mean I want to end our friendship, because I care a lot for you, but I miss seeing other people. What if we back off from each other just a little? Maybe it would be good if I came to your house the next time I feel like having coffee together. The main thing is not seeing each other every single day like we have been. I just need some space."

Without a doubt Alison would feel hurt and rejected, but sometimes we just have to experience those feelings. It's unreasonable to hope we can go through life without feeling hurt and rejected, and we can always learn something when something like that occurs. The ball would now be in Alison's court, and she'd have to look at her options and decide how she wanted to respond.

She might be so hurt she'd distance herself completely and totally reject her old friend. Or she might hear the request and respect her friend's wishes, backing off and seeing what happens. As our neighbor felt the pressure diminish she might relax and begin gradually to view the relationship as more positive than negative. Little by little they could redefine their friendship, both setting boundaries and expressing expectations honestly and respectfully.

To get out of a friendship cage, we begin by accepting our own feelings, being willing to express them with kindness and continuing to relate if we want to maintain a relationship. If we don't, we let go of it and move on, freeing the other person to reach out to others.

To stay stuck in a friendship that is no longer satisfying is disrespectful to ourselves and eventually to the friend as well. Our resentment is almost sure to surface in many ways if we try to ignore it or hide it, and the person whom we're resenting will hear it loud and clear. It becomes an unfair message to send anyone, because it deals them a double disadvantage. They feel the rejection and they also feel confusion. They can't put their finger on it, but they know in their bones things are not right. Their frustration mounts as they try harder to figure out what's wrong, and when they continue receiving mixed messages they become increasingly discouraged.

Honesty with kindness opens the door in that "troubled friendship" cage.

What about other relationship cages? Basically the method is the same. Becoming aware of our feelings, being willing to express them respectfully, and following through with attempts at solutions. Of course the way we try to change the relationship can turn out to be unsatisfying as well. That's okay. That's not failure; it's simply discovering what doesn't work. The more attempts we make, the closer we are to finding a solution that does.

A common cage in which many of us find ourselves is the parent-child cage, and it can imprison in both directions. Many parents feel overly responsible for their grown children, and legions of offspring fret about how to handle their mothers and fathers. Even if we live in widely separated cities we still may feel like one party is the warden, watching and disapproving of our behavior, looking for one false move and waiting to blow the whistle.

Blow the whistle? Just what will they do if we do something of which they disapprove?

Well, they... They...they disapprove, is what they do.

Yeah, and then what?

Well, I can't handle that.

Yeah, so what happens to you?

Well, I hate it, is all, so I try to avoid it.

There is a kind of mutual discomfort in many parent-child relationships, in which both sides are so keenly aware of the other's feelings they don't enjoy each other very much.

I love the story about an old couple who go to their attorney and say in firm but crackly voices, "We want to get a divorce."

"A divorce!" the lawyer responds. "You two have been married a long time; how long?"

"Seventy years," they answer with a certain amount of pride.

"And you want a divorce now? Why now, for goodness sakes, if you've stayed together all these years?"

"We had to wait till the kids died."

We all know couples who seem to resent one another terribly, and sometimes we find ourselves wondering what keeps them together. Maybe now we know the answer.

I know adults who don't smoke in front of their parents, hoping the parents will never have to know. And I know adults who don't smoke in front of their children for the same reason. Both feel somewhat controlled by the other, and their relationship is diminished because of it.

People who are open and honest in every other relationship may be guarded and secretive with their parents. In that sense they're hiding in their cages. Cages always make us feel deprived and punished, so we come to hate them. Anytime we retreat to a cage for safety we're going to pay some stiff consequences. Granted, they may keep us protected from something, but they'll extract a price from us that's a whole lot worse. Again, the solution becomes the problem.

In every living thing is the spirit to be free, and our cages defeat that spirit. We are often our own prison guards, keeping ourselves incarcerated by the very behavior we happened onto years ago in an effort to take care of ourselves.

One client, angry with her husband for leaving her, stayed stuck in feeling depressed. Long after he'd left she remained sad and discouraged, feeling wounded and rejected. In our counseling sessions she saw that she was still trying to punish him. She couldn't let herself be happy and enjoy life for fear that he would then feel "off the hook." Keeping him guilt-ridden was her hidden agenda for making herself remain depressed.

It always helps to look for those hidden agendas when we have a problem we seem unable to lick. We're getting a payoff for holding onto the problem, and once we can recognize it we can decide what we want to do about it. Maybe we want to keep it, and that's okay if it's a decision we make. Had this woman chosen to keep punishing her ex-husband with her depression, she could have done it the rest of her life. The main problem was that it didn't seem to bother him in the slightest.

The more disinterested he was, the more depressed she tried to be. When she realized the dynamics she actually laughed. It took her no time at all, then, to begin to live again. Before long she had a new boyfriend.

Escaping the Cage

How do we know if we're in a cage? Feeling discontented clues us in, and that can range from stirrings of boredom all the way to deep depression. In almost every case unhappiness indicates a cage of some kind, and often a whole series of cages. We shuffle from one to another and back again, looking for relief, seeking a magic answer but almost never being able to experience joy for any length of time.

Sometimes in our discouragement we turn to drugs and lay a foundation for still another cage. Drugs can be any mind-altering substance, even coffee. Researchers tell us that a glass of wine a day might be good for us physically, but in some of us it can become an out-of-control addiction. A beer can become a six-pack a day and then a twelve-pack, and then add a few shots of vodka and we're looking at alcoholism.

Does that mean we shouldn't drink? Not necessarily, though we should be wary if there is a history of alcoholism in the family. The day will soon be here when babies can be tested for the gene that makes them susceptible to the disease, and if it's present they might do well not to test their tolerance. Still, that's got to be their decision.

But even if we're not "official" alcoholics we can develop drinking problems if we use alcohol to fuzzy up the rough spots in our living. That's how addictions begin—finding something pleasant to take our minds away from our discontent. Be it a thumb, a cigarette or a beer, it's our solution that may become the problem.

Food is certainly a common cage. My chocolate-addicted friend says, "The bars on my cage are candy bars. I can't get through a day without them. I crave them for the sugar high they give me, and when the low hits I have to eat another. It's what I do all day long. I hate myself for it, but it's a need that's so strong it defeats me. I absolutely cannot stop."

She's now attending Overeaters Anonymous and learning that sugar is a luxury she can't afford. Her system uses it exactly like alcohol, and one taste of sugar to her is like one drink to the alcoholic. Even refined flour turns quickly to sugar in the system, so her whole diet is affected.

So what does she have to do? I prefer seeing it as a choice she gets to make, not one she has to make.

She can decide whether her cage is so unpleasant that she's willing to change her behavior and leave it. For her that would mean skipping anything with sugar in it. For the rest of her life? Perhaps so. Is it worth it? Only she can decide. If the sugar cage is more pleasant to her than her life would be outside, she may sentence herself back in.

The bad news is that it means giving up a habit that's become terribly precious to her. The good news is she'll become free again, able to feel in charge of her life. It's been a lot of years since she woke up in the morning feeling really good. Instead, her waking up has been a groggy, depressed feeling of self-hatred, dreading another day, wishing she could do without the chocolate and yet checking her kitchen cupboard immediately to make sure she has her stock of candy bars ready and waiting. And loathing her weakness.

She may have to play around with the decision for a while, maybe for quite a long while. Many times we decide to quit a habit, and we actually step outside the cage and taste the freedom. But especially in substance abuse, where there is actually a physical withdrawal that can be highly uncomfortable, we may decide it isn't worth it and rush back into the cage for a quick fix.

However, realizing that you're the boss of you gives you a sense of power. Nobody can make you quit using chocolate or nicotine if you don't want to. You can defeat anyone who tries to get you to stop drinking or smoking. Give up a sick relationship because somebody tells you to? No way. You will stop only if you decide it's worth the effort.

Perhaps it helps to look at your life as your story; your play, or a movie you're making about yourself.

You're the script writer. You get to write your story any way you please. And you can have as many rehearsals as you want in order to make the scene come out the way want it. If you flub it once or twenty times or a hundred times you just keep practicing, perhaps revising your script and repeating "takes" until you like it.

You may decide to change your relationship with the cast members if they're a problem. If you want to stop drinking and all your friendships revolve around partying, you may choose to recast your movie and find some new friends who are not so bent on booze. That isn't an easy transition and may take a little time. Meanwhile you'll probably feel like a lost lamb, missing the friends who were so important to you and lonely because you've not yet found replacements.

That's the period during which we're tempted to rush back into the cage. It calls for a tremendous amount of courage to leave our various cages and even more to stay away from them. If all our behavior is geared toward either pursuing pleasure or avoiding pain we can understand how the cages seemed to meet our needs. They served one of those goals and maybe both.

But they don't anymore, or we wouldn't see them as problem areas in our lives. Now we get to make a conscious decision about them, however, and take care of ourselves. Do we leave them or do we stay?

Whichever decision we make needn't be permanent, of course. We might want to get out of one of our cages but stay a while in the others; there's no need to do everything at once. Knowing I can change my mind anytime along the way helps me relax about the whole thing.

Actually we're already half in and half out of some of them anyway. One of my strong focuses has always been comfort, pure creature comfort. It's inordinately important to me to feel good at all times. I lean toward jeans, cotton socks and underwear, big loose sweaters and comfortable shoes. I hate being hungry or thirsty or cold or hot. To be tired is a condition I avoid at all costs. After a good night's sleep the world is my oyster, and I sail through the day joyously. After a bad night even my family prefers to be wherever I'm not.

In other words, comfort sometimes is a cage that protects me but also deprives me of fun I might be having.

Our friends Beth and Chuck went on a one-day cruise from San Diego to Ensenada, Mexico, and came back glowing. I listened with eagerness as Beth described the wonderful meals. I made her tell me about all the desserts. I loved hearing about the sights and the shops in Mexico. I was almost ready to get Larry and drive to San Diego so we could take that cruise when Beth said, "We had to be on board on seven in the morning and we got home around midnight."

My face fell as I thought, "Oh no, what a long day! I'd have to be up at the crack of dawn, and exhausted by ten o'clock. The last two hours would be miserable. No, I guess I'd better just forget the whole thing."

I realize I'm letting my comfort cage keep me from an experience that could be terrific. So, okay, I can live my life without a one-day cruise. But I'm disappointed in myself for letting comfort be so important to me. If I continue that way it's only a matter of time before I become practically a recluse, shut up in my house where I have everything exactly the way I like it. No trips; traveling tires one. No plays; they get out late. Try a new experience? It might be uncomfortable. Take a class? Have a dinner party? Oh, better not; it's a lot of work.

So I see my comfort priority as potentially damaging, and I'm struggling a bit to free myself of its clutches. If I don't I'll end up a weak, wimpy fat old woman who simply lies on a soft couch and eats and hates myself—not a pretty sight. It's not quite a cage yet, to me, but it's a very seductive lifestyle that could easily become one.

Perhaps I'm fortunate to have vanity as another strong focus. I hate being overweight, so I make myself walk and exercise some, and I watch my diet obsessively. The desire to look as good as I can might keep me from staying in that cage of creature comforts.

On the other hand, vanity itself can be a cage! My friend Marie won't leave her house unless she's dressed perfectly and freshly made up, with every hair in place. She wouldn't dream of playing a game of tennis because then she'd look all disheveled and sweaty. She may not ever marry because she says, "I never want a man to see me unless I look perfect."

Her physical perfectionism is a cage as crippling as any addiction. Just about anything can become a cage.

Another friend has worked very hard to create a beautiful home, and it is truly a showplace. Each time I visit I'm impressed with new additions, elegant landscaping, the most expensive furniture and carpet you sink into with every footstep. Every inch is immaculate. One day she confessed with a little chuckle, "You know, Lee, sometimes I wish I could live in a little bitty house in the back yard. I could keep this house perfect that way, and I wouldn't worry about what the little house looked like."

But you and I can guess what would happen to the little bitty house: it would get fixed up and added onto, cleaned from top to bottom and professionally decorated before long. It would become still another cage, and she'd have to move into a third little bitty house.

Creating cages seems innate in us. Give us a problem and we'll cast about to find ourselves a solution. Once we have it we'll feel so good about it we'll immerse ourselves in it, giving it so much of our energy that before we know it we've made ourselves a fine cage. That's normal, everyday behavior.

So if you can think of a cage in your life, rejoice! It means you're human like everybody else. If you have two or three or more, pat yourself on the back for being so creative in your problem solving. I have several myself, perhaps looking like a row of "Porta-Potties" at a construction site or a carnival.

Wine became one to me years ago, and I clung to that one for quite a while before I abandoned it. After several years I decided to treat myself with *one* glass of wine a day, and I will not go beyond that. It works.

You may want to keep your cages if they're not doing more harm than good. Why change your life if it's working well for you? However, if you find them keeping you from a happier lifestyle, you get to look around and find that door that's always open. Maybe you want to move from one cage to another for now and live in that one for a while. Or perhaps you'll consider "camping out" and trying life outside them.

The main thing is not to get discouraged if you find yourself running back for comfort. It seems we need to run back many times, each time re-discovering the unhappiness our cages cause us. Finally one day we feel ourselves consciously aware we don't need them anymore.

Like a toddler who finds he can sleep without his baby blanket, we get to feel the tremendous high of knowing we've outgrown a habit we wanted to kick. Few things in life make us prouder than confronting a problem and licking it. Our self-esteem rises impressively.

But don't be hard on yourself if you're not ready yet. Trying to teach a toddler to ride a trike when she's not ready is an impossible task that frustrates everyone involved. Suddenly she reaches the proper readiness level and off she rides, easy as pie. When you're ready, you're ready, and you know it. Still you can give it a shot every now and then and see how your level is, like the child who may climb onto the trike many times before being able to ride it.

Meanwhile, feel pleased just to recognize your cage or cages and come to accept them as important parts of your growing up. You needed them once or you wouldn't have built them, and it's always tough to give up an aspect of our lives that was positive to us for a while.

Cages are kind of like high school: fun, sometimes exciting and dramatic, filling many of our needs, teaching us so much, and enhancing our lives tremendously. Often we sign one another's yearbook with more than little tugs of pain as we realize we're saying goodbye to an era. We may think, "Is there life after high school?" But now, as adults, who of us would want to go back?

Life has been so full of other choices since then; we look back at high school with fond nostalgia and move on.

Our cages can be the same. Let's enjoy them while we choose to live in them and know we get to free ourselves when we're ready.

Do we all have a cage or two? Or four or five? I think virtually everyone does. We may have moved out of some cages in the past, but probably moved into a couple of new ones since then. Since they're so easy to find when we're troubled, and so comforting to call home, we'd have to be extraordinarily strong not to inhabit them.

I already mentioned leaving cages of my past, albeit only temporarily in case I wanted them back. But I was surprised when I discovered I'd unwillingly stepped into a new one when I learned I was a glommer.

Glomming itself is a cage. Just as a thumb becomes a pleasant cage for a baby, and food becomes one to a lonely or troubled man or woman, so a love relationship can become one to a person who, guided by the laws of nature, falls in love.

It's natural to get hungry and need food. It's just as natural to seek a mate. In both cases the desire is a result of the way we're made and our basic drives of self preservation and continuing the human race. Both are God-given gifts.

Both, however, can so easily become cages if we make them too important in our lives. Often they take the place of solving some other problem we're facing.

As one who savors my one daily glass of wine I admire people who can drink two or three and have no wish to drink more. Alcoholics Anonymous teaches that "one drink is too many, and a thousand aren't enough." We always wish we could have more.

I envy folks who are totally content after one glass of wine or a handful of corn chips, because I'm stopping there only because of a strong desire *not* to fall victim to more and more and more again.

In college I would buy a large bag of Fritos and eat the whole thing, though my lips would be hurting from the excess of salt and my mind would be reminding me I simply must stop eating them.

Over the years I've developed an impressive ability to listen to my reasonable mind and stop eating and/or drinking. That obedience to myself has formed only after a zillion mornings of hating myself as I read the morning scale. Vanity plays a huge role as well. I don't like having a sticky-out tummy, and I can maintain a flat one only by depriving myself of excesses. Mind you, I'm never depriving myself of a balanced three squares a day—only the excesses.

How do I know I'm in a glommer's cage? Being a glommer makes me unhappy. I dislike not being happy. I want to feel content most of the time, and most of the time I do, the main exception being when

I focus on what's missing in my life: a close, loving relationship.

I have a husband who is a good man. He supports me financially; he does his share of home and yard maintenance. He's esteemed in the community as an eager helper of needy causes. He's nice looking and extremely bright. I see all those traits and appreciate them. So what's wrong?

He places me quite low on his preferred activity list. He'd rather be many other places instead of with me. He prefers other people to me. He's not very interested in what I'm telling him. In a nutshell, I'm just not as important to him as I'd like to be.

So he's not The Prince who married Cinderella, or The Lover seen in a lifetime of movies who wanted nothing more than The Woman.

And that is my cage.

When I emerge from that cage and do something enjoyable, I become happy again. Content. What I want in life, right? I have a lot of interests and a few real talents that transport me to a totally different state of being in which I can lose myself for hours on end. But I have to exit my cage in order to do them.

Probably the most important road I took (other than marrying and having four children whom I adore) was returning to school at age forty to learn how to be a marriage and family counselor. Those couple of years studying the mind why it acts the way it does, were totally fascinating to me, and I was entranced the entire time.

I cried the day I graduated, recognizing what pleasures I was leaving. Now that I think about it, continuing university work could have become still another cage: a place with a set of activities that fed me and kept me happy.

I can see I was fortunate in my eagerness to get a license and begin a private practice that lasted for 35 years. (Goody. One cage I did *not* enter.) But the glommer cage is still an unwelcome factor in my life that I often find myself occupying after all these years.

five

Another Epiphany

"I'm really fed up with the resentment that I carry around all the time," I began. "It does me absolutely no good; on the contrary, it causes me a great deal of harm, and yet I haven't been able to let go of it."

Fifteen years ago I was beginning a private session with Tom Condon, one of the highly recognized authors and educators in the Enneagram movement, after attending his workshop entitled "Personal Change." We'd spent two days looking at the nine personality styles: their strengths, their weaknesses, and how we can focus on making them work more positively in our lives.

I'd arranged for this personal session because I was frustrated with my inability to take care of this ongoing problem of mine, my holding tightly to a quiet anger I'd been entertaining for too many years.

Keenly aware of the importance of forgiving, I preached it in my practice as a marriage, family and individual therapist. I believed strongly in the importance of independence as opposed to a dependent way of living.

I knew I'd been too emotionally dependent all my life, even though I'd seen the error of my ways through counseling in my thirties. That's when I returned to school for a master's degree in counseling and guidance. Since then I'd been in private practice for some twenty-five years, written three self-help books, and given hundreds of presentations on "how to be happy."

Wanting to be honest, however, I always admitted in my writings and my lectures that my tendency to wish for "the undying attention of a prince in a castle" still caused me some grief. I could laugh at myself easily as I disclosed that unfortunate fact, but it still rankled and caused me too much frustration.

Almost daily something would remind me that my forty-six-year marriage wasn't what I'd hoped it would be.

I knew I was married to a good guy, honest as the day is long, bright and articulate, kind, thoughtful, and generous to everyone. Ah, but that's the rub. The "generous to everyone" part. Indeed, Larry is so glad to fill the wants and needs of every person he meets there's little time left for us to be together.

He's widely known in Tucson and Arizona, with affiliations in dozens of clubs and organizations throughout the state. He has friends and acquaintances in every walk of life. He has a passion for watching sports of any kind, a powerful love of the Catholic faith, a genuine interest and loyalty to our alma mater, Northern Arizona University, and a continuing involvement in radio and television, the profession from which he "retired" a few years ago.

In all those areas he remains enthusiastically active, attending meetings with the zeal of a little kid in Disneyland. He joins new boards and committees as easily as most of us might attend a movie, and, once a member, he wouldn't dream of skipping an event except for a serious reason.

From time to time there is a conflict, of course, when two of his organizations are meeting at the same time, and he looks as stricken as if the ultimate success of the group vitally depends on his presence.

I blush to admit I've been known to make snide remarks when that occurs; something like, "Oh yeah, the whole Muscular Dystrophy Association will have to fold if you miss a meeting." Actually I know he doesn't see himself as necessary for the group's success, but rather that he made a commitment and commitments must be honored.

When I complain that I never get to see him he cheerfully recommends that I put a time and date on the calendar and he will honor it. And so I do, for maybe three weeks down the road, or his first available time slot. But inwardly I frown. Okay, generally the frown is outward.

I know it's because I'm still visualizing my lifelong dream of How Life Is Supposed To Be, According To Lee. It's supposed to be a glomming together of two romantic people, both eternally enchanted with the other, enjoying endless sharing of thoughts and feelings and experiences delightful to each. Isn't it?

Well, no, I guess I know it can't really be that way. And I have to admit that there have been many times when we're together that we both look uncomfortably blank regarding the question, "So what shall we do?"

Unfortunately we have few interests in common.

Fortunately, however, we have many interests that we individually enjoy. So it's not that I must sit here looking out the window like a child having to stay inside because she has a cold, longing to be out there playing.

On the contrary, my happiest times are probably when I'm being creative in some way. I love to make beautiful things like slipcovers, clothes to wear, jewelry, art, crafty gifts, decorations or any kind of home decor.

I become so absorbed when I'm making something lovely that I have no need to feel sorry for myself. In fact I'm downright happy! Same as when I'm writing an article, or a book, or e-mailing my friends and family.

So why, then, do I spend some time every day wishing things were different—"things," of course, really meaning "Larry."

If wishing could have changed him he'd have made that remarkable transformation years ago, I know. And goodness knows I did way more than simply wish. I talked probably hundreds of hours on the subject, dipping into every kind of communication I could think of.

I could write a book on "A Thousand Ways to Try to Change Your Mate," and it might actually become a best-seller, but the horrible secret it would deliberately omit is this: none of those ways work. One can't change one's mate. To be sure, one's mate can change, but only if he chooses to, and all the wheedling, reasoning, scolding, weeping and railing one performs are virtually useless.

Certainly I've known that for dozens of years. I teach it, I preach it, I write it. And yet, in my heart of hearts, there lingers the sad little voice that says, "But I wish it were different."

Along with that has been a good bit of resentment that I've made quite clear to Larry.

Perhaps I should write a second book entitled, "A Thousand Ways to Show Your Resentment When Your Mate Doesn't Change." Most of them everyone already knows, I suspect. You've got your silent treatment, your obvious smoldering, your disinterest in sex, your sarcasm, your refusal to laugh at his jokes, your cleverly subtle ways of putting him down, making him feel inadequate, your criticism of his friends-organizations-interests-hobbies-appearance, and those are just for starters.

It takes a lot of work to keep up these methods, goodness knows. Keeping resentment alive is not for the weak of spirit! You have to work at it, and that takes a tremendous amount of energy.

But I'm proud to say I kept it up for many years with finely honed skill and unfailing consistency. Oh, I had my share of diseases over the years that may have been caused because of the stress resentment causes in one's physical self, but I withstood them with undaunted determination! No wimp I.

Determined though I was, however, I certainly wasn't happy with the way things were.

So it was that I sat with Tom Condon that evening after the workshop, looking for insight into why I was hanging on to a habit that had become so tiresome. I knew I wanted to let it go, but why had I been unable to all these years?

Tom's first suggestion was, "Give me three reasons why you're reluctant to give up the resentment you feel toward Larry."

Hoo! That was a surprise, and difficult to do. I hadn't ever really looked for reasons to hold onto it, but I did think of one.

"I guess one is that it would let Larry off the hook," I said, and I had to laugh at that, a hollow and nervously embarrassed laugh.

I continued. "It doesn't seem fair that he gets off scot free while I'm the one who has to do the adapting. He thinks we have a great marriage and that I'm unrealistic in wishing it were still romantic."

Tom has a way of gently joking with his clients, not in an unkind or critical way, but in a manner that's affectionate and indulgent.

"Oh, yeah, you don't want to ever quit punishing him," he said in pseudo soberness. "After all, if you punish him long enough and hard enough he might start loving you again."

He pauses for a few seconds, and then he smiles broadly and warmly.

Of course he made me laugh. I mean I knew it was futile to punish, but I kept finding myself doing it. Just to make sure he knew I was less than happy. (Forty-six years into the marriage he must have had a pretty good grasp of it by then.)

My second reason was, "It would mean letting go of a lifelong dream. I always thought marriage was supposed to be romantic and intimate." Clearly I didn't want to change that expectation, even if it was unrealistic. I felt like "I know how I want our relationship to be, and Larry should want that, too." If I produced an endless barrage of information on that subject, surely someday he'd see the light. Right? Wrong.

His response was always to say, "I just can't make you happy," and go on about his business.

Tom said, "I see a little girl inside you who is really strong and stubborn. She has dug her heels in the ground, her arms are crossed, and she's grimly determined to make Larry see life the way she sees it. She can't do that, of course, but she's sure not going to give up trying."

I had to laugh again, because I knew he was right. I knew that little girl, and she was a spunky, relentless, and tenacious child who was hell-bent on getting her way.

I didn't really like her much, but I respected and admired her unflagging persistence. I had no choice but to agree with Tom's appraisal.

He said, "If that were a real little girl controlling your life that much, would you put up with it?"

No way. I'd have to be crazy to let her push me around.

"What would you tell her when she tried to control you?" he asked.

I thought for a moment.

"I'd smile at her and say, 'Go away, kid. I've got other things to think about, other things to do.' Then I'd shoo her out and go about my business."

Tom asked, "What are you doing when you're most aware of feeling sad and resentful?"

I replied, "Pretty much nothing. It's usually when I'm idle, maybe just lying in bed in the morning, or being bored. When I'm focused on something I don't even think about it. In fact I'm happiest when I'm being creative in some way: painting or sewing or writing, something like that."

"So you know how to change your focus the next time you begin feeling that way?"

"I do," I assured him. "I really think I've gotten all I needed from you this time, Tom. I want to get rid of the resentment once and for all. Larry's never going to change; probably he can't change. I just want to accept him for who he is and keep my life happy with things I like to do."

I felt remarkably free. I was lighthearted and grateful as I paid Tom's well-deserved fee. What he said was not really new information to me, but the way he offered it struck some kind of chord in me that was different.

I drove home feeling giddy and euphoric, eager to see Larry and tell him about my hour.

Needless to say he was interested and fascinated, and, while he looked pleased for me, there was an understandable reserve in his face. Almost as if he were thinking, "This is too good to be true. She's just fresh from that session, and she feels that way now, but it can't last."

That was okay. I didn't need him to feel my firm resolution. What mattered was my certainty that it was there and things were going to be different.

That night I had two dreams. Having learned in one of my classes that all the roles in a person's dreams reflect different facets of the person himself, I tried that out with my first dream.

It was one in which I was doing some work in my home when the doorbell rang. Outside stood a little girl who reminded me of a real child who used to live across the alley from us. She was about eight or nine but very confident and adult, and she seemed "street wise." Her mom gave her a lot of freedom and space, obviously, because she'd be out and about the neighborhood until quite late at night, chatting with anyone who'd take the time. Her name was Bo.

In my dream she had a friend with her and asked if they could both come and visit. Reluctantly I let them in, though I was a bit put out at having my work interrupted, but I did feel some sense of compassion for her.

She introduced her friend, Emily, who seemed shy; she was hanging back a bit timidly, not knowing who I was or what to expect. Bo started showing her around our house while I continued cleaning the kitchen.

The doorbell rang again and it was a third girl, Mindy, a stranger to me as well, but Bo let her in and began giving her a tour as well, talking to her animatedly and comfortably.

After a few minutes little Emily came to me in the kitchen and, on the verge of tears, asked if I could please take her home. Bo was paying attention only to Mindy, and Emily felt very left out and alone.

Understanding how it hurts to feel left out and lonely I agreed to take her home, but now I was really annoyed. Why had I let Bo intrude on my space, bringing in strangers to whom I now needed to cater! I felt angry but tried to hide it so Emily wouldn't feel even worse.

Bo and Mindy went about the house, checking everything out, enjoying themselves, and I took Emily out to my car. Then I woke up.

I lay there thinking about it for a while and remembered what I'd learned in class, so I tried on the roles of all three girls as well as myself.

As Bo I felt entitled to do whatever I wanted to do. So confident was I that I didn't bat an eye at imposing myself and my friends on whatever hapless acquaintance I happened upon. My thoughts would have gone like this: "I like myself and I like everybody else, and it's perfectly all right to ask whatever I want of them. I fully believe they're going to give me whatever it is I want, and we'll all be happy."

Yes, I admit, there is a part of me who feels like that. Like "I'm a good person who likes to do nice things for others, so they should do nice things for me as well." (Interpretation: If I like spending time with Larry, he should like spending time with me.)

As Emily I didn't want to be brought to this house by Bo. My thoughts: "Well, I guess I'd better go along with Bo even though I don't know this lady, and I don't want to go into this strange house. I thought Bo and I were just going to play together, but I didn't count on this strange activity, and I'm nervous about it." (Interpretation: I like one-on-one time. I look forward to the intimacy of just two best friends enjoying each other. I don't want to be just one of a group.)

As Mindy, "I can always count on Bo to lead me into new and exciting adventures. She just went into that lady's house, so I'll go see what they're doing. I'd never do that alone, but with Bo as my friend I'm sure I'll be more than welcome." (Interpretation: It's fun to do new things and have adventures, especially with someone I really like!)

And as myself, "Darn these kids! Mostly I'm mad at myself for being too wimpy to say no and just close the door. I wouldn't have had to be mean about it, just a smile and pleasant 'Not right now, Bo,' would have worked fine. I'm always letting people intrude and use up my precious time. I'm not taking care of myself and my needs, and I know it's my own stupid fault that I'm 'entertaining' guests I don't want. Now I have to be responsible for taking this kid home and leaving the others alone in my house. What a bummer. I'm furious but I don't dare show it. It's so unfair! I'm victimized again." (Interpretation: I am truly my worst enemy. I let others take control of my life, and then I resent what they do and how it impacts me. Even worse is being too wimpy to be assertive and say what I want. I'm still too afraid of disapproval. When am I going to learn?)

I had to smile at the resemblance of my dream and the "little child" within me, recognizing there are more than one—maybe even more than three or four.

I went back to sleep and dreamed again.

This time I was going to a home in the Hollywood Hills where there was a yellow convertible sports car in the garage that was to come to me. How that occurred wasn't addressed, but I had a vague impression that my husband had left it there for safe keeping until I could come and drive it home.

The house owner was a man named Dick who made me feel very unwelcome. Clearly he was unhappy that I was there for my car.

When I awoke I tried on both roles as I had before and uncovered two very genuine parts of my personality:

As Dick I'd think to myself, "Here is this foolish woman who wants that car. I've taken such good care of it and kept it in mint condition, and now she thinks she can waltz in here and just drive it out of my life! I'm sure she won't even be able to get it down these curvy roads without crashing into something and ruining it completely. I don't want to let her do it! I won't let her do it! I don't trust her to care for it as I have."

As Lee I thought, "This cute little yellow car is rightfully mine, and I'm going to drive it out of here if I have to run over this clown in the process. He can't prevent me from taking what's mine." Determinedly I stood my ground, insisting Dick give me the keys and open his garage door.

Dick: This woman's a real threat to me. She's right, of course; it is her car, and I have no choice but to let her take it, but I'm going to warn her that she can't handle it. I'll do my darnedest to prevent her from taking it. I'm the careful, perfectionist person who's kept it so beautifully, and this snippet plans to pull rank and drive it out? I don't think so! (Interpretation: I have my life planned carefully to keep everything safe. Even if I'm not particularly happy I don't want to risk changing anything. I've spent years doing it this way, I'm used to it, and I want to keep it that way.)

Lee: I won't be pushed around by anybody! I've been too wimpy too long, and from now I take charge of my own life. Furthermore it's going to give me a lot of pleasure to whip this car around the curves and burn out of here, knowing how he's hating it. (Interpretation: I'm ready for the new me to take over. I'm through with the old weak, timid me, and I'm going to use this new strength and determination to enrich my life. Stand back, everybody; you're gonna see some fast driving!)

In both dreams I saw clearly how fed up I was with maintaining the status quo. I wanted to get rid of the dependent, emotionally needy person and take over my life as the strong, capable woman I knew I am. I became determined to stop wishing others would change and quit wallowing in self-pity about their behavior.

I had the right to "drive the cute little yellow sports car" on my own, and no one, not even me, could stop me.

It was definitely an epiphany. No longer feeling like the helpless, ineffectual victim, I knew with certainty I had turned a corner and was headed down a different street. No matter that I didn't know where it would lead; I was eager to go find out for myself, and there wasn't a shred of doubt that I'd be able to handle whatever challenges I might encounter.

Furthermore, now that I'd been freed from the prison to which I'd willingly sentenced myself, I could stop feeling anger at the guards. No guard, no "little girl," no cranky caretaker could stop me now, so I could let myself relax and maybe even enjoy those folks.

Not needing anything from them anymore let me quit fighting them, however ineffectually it had been anyway.

With a lightness that felt incredibly easy, I accepted them simply as fellow travelers, not enemies. We could travel down the same roads or not, spend time together if we felt like it, or go separately to wherever we wanted. Mainly I knew I no longer needed them to want to play with me.

The night I gave up that particular dependency was one of my most shining hours, and I knew in my very soul I was different.

I wasn't naive, however. I know too well how our best intentions often have setbacks, and we face what feels like failure many times over. But if we have a game plan for handling those relapses we know what to do. In my case it will be to do almost anything, having recognized that my pity parties occur when I'm idle.

Knowing I'm happiest when I'm engrossed in something creative, I can always pick up my water colors and a brush and lose my melancholy without even trying.

Conversely I also have the option of staying gloomy! By now it's a habit with which I'm so familiar that it has an element of comfort about it; like being with an old friend. I might decide to stay with that for a while, as long as I feel like it, be it five minutes or an hour.

I could enhance the sadness by putting on a CD of songs from the late forties and early fifties, my high school and college years, when romance was really happening. I can hear Slow Boat to China and be right back there at a dance in the gym, excited at being with a certain boy. Dream takes me back to the many "last dances" of the evening, when it would soon be time to leave with the "boyfriend du jour" and ride around Winslow until I had to be home.

Parking on a little hill to talk and kiss and hug and murmur made us just about die of passion and desire, intensified by our morals of those years: you had to save sex for marriage. Nothing was more of an aphrodisiac than that! The radio might be playing "I Wish I Didn't Love You So," and the night air was cool and fresh, and the whole scene was absolute perfection.

I can transport myself back there in a heartbeat and savor the nostalgia any time I want. But it's laced with an almost inevitable poignant wistfulness that serves only to feed my state of gloom.

Imagination can be frighteningly powerful. Focusing on what we wish "could be" can really get us sidetracked onto a dangerous and painful dead-end street. Of course it would be lovely to have the absence of wrinkles I had then, and the twenty-four-inch waist.

But I'm way happier focusing on how my life is better now than it was then. I was a bundle of angst in those days, with too little confidence, not much courage, and virtually no wisdom; in other words extremely fragile and insecure.

Now I get to enjoy the certainty that I can stand anything that comes down the pike. I have strength and patience and confidence and a lot of wisdom. The fact that I have droopy jowls and squinty eyes and a thirty-two-inch waist isn't that important anymore.

So I prefer to focus not on what life was like as a teenager, but on all the wonderful facets of how it is now.

The romantic is still a big part of me, and one I want to keep. Romance can take many forms, however. In addition to the love-intimacy part that the word usually implies, it includes creativity, optimism, fancy, imagination, idealism, philosophy, sensitivity, and love of the arts. My favorite facet is probably the intensity. I relish the depth of sensation I can explore, even though sometimes it's negative.

I often find a dessert "the best I ever tasted in my whole life," and a bad movie "a horrible, wretched waste of two hours, every minute of which I loathed." I'm almost never lukewarm.

Being aware of the little girls who share my mind and body gives me a new point of concentration. I can get a big kick out of attending to each one of them, but knowing I'm in control of them, not vice versa.

Most of the time I want to be the confident, comfortable, in-charge "Bo," unafraid, secure and unflappable.

But sometimes I want to be the dependent, needy little person who wants to lean on someone. Not for long, though. I can also be the follower who just goes along with the others, not needing to control, but being a willing participant in other people's plans.

I don't want to banish any of those children. But I do intend to keep myself as the "camp director" who chooses which one gets to be the leader at a particular time.

As a primarily Adlerian therapist I've long known the value of seeking out the "payoff" in holding onto a specific problem. Often it takes a little searching to find the fulfillment before we can help the client discover why he refuses give it up. Tom Condon did that in his "Give me three reasons for being unwilling to let it go."

But adding the stubborn little girl to the picture gave it a clarity that I hadn't recognized in myself. It put me in the driver's seat, enabling me to take the power in my life and not feel victimized and stuck in an unhealthy, blaming position. I don't want to be there anymore.

That ship has sailed. It looks wonderful disappearing into the sunset!

Fifteen Years Later

Okay, I must confess that the ship that had sailed has sailed right back to my beach many times since that great epiphany. I have to keep turning it around and sending it back out to sea, and I'm sick of it.

I should break a bottle of champagne on it and christen the ship *Poor Dear Lee*, shouldn't I? It's my old beloved cage which I welcome back with tenderness because we've been so close for so long.

Even though I welcome it back with comfortable sentimentality, it isn't here long before I remember how much grief it causes me. How simple and free my life is when the ship is far away. I never even miss it.

Why on earth, then, do I let it back when it docks at the bay? I need to recognize it as an old friend who has taken advantage of my hospitality way too many times already. It's robbed me, it's lied to me, it's betrayed me, it's disappointed me in every way I can imagine, and I've sent it away each time with great relief and determination not to let it in, should it ever return.

Then it does, and what do I do? I *welcome* it! I feed it and give it shelter for the hundredth time. The world's dumbest idiot would know better, wouldn't you think?

It may look like a ship, but it's really the familiar old cage. By now it's chipped and dented, with some broken bars hanging down; a sorry-looking contraption designed to make me sad.

Since it's all about my relationship with my husband I need to re-define that. The relationship, not the cage/ship.

I've learned to re-define items of clothing, like a brightly flowered A-line dress I made and loved for several years. After so many washings and dryings it became "tired" looking, and I couldn't enjoy wearing it out in public anymore, but I suddenly saw it as a great nightgown; old and soft and nice enough when nobody from the outside world would see it.

What was not acceptable as a dress anymore made a perfect nightgown. A couple of Larry's dress shirts that had seen better days became good shirts for me to paint in. It's just a matter of changing their purpose.

If it works for clothing it should work for anything, shouldn't it?

The intimacy and romance I longed for most of my life has not materialized in my marriage, but the marriage itself has many other benefits. When I get up in the morning I smell coffee already made, and the morning paper is lying on my place mat.

When I go to the grocery store I buy whatever supplies we need without a thought of whose checkbook it's coming from (Larry's). We have a good division of labor and of finances. He pays for food, shelter, and insurance. I pay for indoor furniture, flooring, drapes, and any decorating I want. We each buy and maintain our own cars. It's a system we both like, simple and effective. He opens jars I can't budge, and I buy all his clothes.

I trust him in every department. In so many practical ways he's a perfect husband. If I didn't have the expectation and wish that we could "talk for hours" I know I'd say I have a fine marriage.

It seems pretty simple, then, doesn't it? I just need to change my expectations *permanently*! We all have imperfections we wouldn't have chosen, but we learn to accept them. We either accept them or we make ourselves miserable hating them.

It's my choice. I get to decide. Again.

Now that we've established the fact that people do *not* change unless they really want to, I'd like to share with you some helpful ways to go about understanding ourselves more clearly. The more intimately we know ourselves, the more knowledge we gather as to methods of self change that will work the most effectively for us. We're such conglomerations of DNA, lifestyle decisions we made as children, family values, priorities, morals, and expectations, that each of us must (or rather, gets to) discover by trial and error what works best for us.

six

You're The Star

Suppose you had a long, long movie about your life up to this very minute. Let's say it's on DVD so you can pop it into your player and watch it anytime you want. It would no doubt take dozens of discs or maybe even hundreds, depending on your age, but they could all be labeled and dated so you could choose one from any period of your life, fix yourself a bowl of popcorn and settle back to be entertained. Wouldn't that be wonderful?!

Some of the discs would be more worn than others, because probably you'd have watched your favorite incidents many times. You could relive the golden moments, complete with sound and the original cast.

It might sometimes be painful to watch, even the happy times. Maybe especially the happy times. Looking back at precious moments that we took for granted at the time could render us choked with sadness as we viewed them now. We'd have the advantage of age and wisdom to point up the magnificence that we didn't recognize then, and the knowledge that those times can never be recaptured.

Like Emily in Thornton Wilder's <u>Our Town</u>, we might weep at our innocence then, our naïveté in having thought things would always be the same.

But we could pick and choose, according to our mood, watching segments that would make us laugh if we felt like it, or make us proud of a particular achievement. We might want to watch just to see how we looked at a certain age, or see how our parents looked when they were the age we are now. We could show our own children how we dressed on our first day of school, and what we ate in the cafeteria for lunch. We could watch our temper tantrums or our deliberate holding in of feelings.

We'd learn how we developed our manipulative skills and who taught them to us by example. We could easily discover why we're good at some subjects and bad at others, possibly in direct proportion to the amount of praise or criticism we received when we attempted them.

What fun it would be to go back to first dates and awkward kisses, to touchdowns and missed touchdowns. To graduations, new jobs, weddings, babies, everything life has given us up to now.

Certainly there would be lots of pain as we watched the replay of the tragedies in our lives. Hopefully we wouldn't play those parts over and over. We'd recognize them, wince, watch them with the appropriate feelings of regret and be relieved to move onto happier scenes.

Or would we?

Actually our viewing habits would reflect the way we choose to live right now. Of course it seems logical to prefer focusing on the positive aspects of our life, and yet why do we so often direct our energies to the negativity of the past?

You probably know people whose entire present seems to be made up of the past, and frequently it's all negative. It's like they push "fast forward" when they get to a good happening and watch with relish all the bad. Furthermore they want us to watch all those downers with them, often in slow motion so we get the full impact of how awful it really was. You know the type.

"Oh, yes, I was married before," they say grimly. "I should have known it wouldn't work. He was the most selfish man that ever walked the earth." Then they wiggle in eager anticipation as they begin long descriptions of each injustice served them. It doesn't matter that we give sympathy and agree with them—that isn't enough. They go on and on with incident number 27, 43, 596. They have a vast wealth of memories of life's rotten moments and a penchant for sharing them with anyone who will listen. Their desire is for everyone else to hate that son-of-a-gun like they do. Should they eventually run out of damning material they can easily switch to another persecutor and go on forever. Eventually they wonder why they have no friends, but then that fact serves as more proof to the world of how unfairly they're treated.

"Do you think one person came to visit me when I was in the hospital?" they wail. "Even my wife has left me!" And you find yourself wanting to join her, wherever she is—away from this tiresome whiner, that's for sure.

Even as I'm chuckling about that kind of behavior I must confess I've done my share of complaining about other people. I remember going to my office one day and popping in to visit Beth, my colleague. I launched into a complaint about my husband, Larry, and Beth listened patiently for a few minutes. Then she asked, "How long has he been that way?"

Delighted with her interest, I said, "Oh, forever! As long as we've been married! Forty-three years!" There was triumph in my voice. Surely she was seeing what a jerk my husband was!

"What makes you think he's ever to going to change?" she asked. "It sounds like you've mentioned it to him numerous times."

"You've got that right!" I stated with righteous indignation.

"So maybe you need to change your expectations instead of wishing he would change his behavior."

"Oh," I said in a small voice, and retreated to my office.

I tell this simply to demonstrate how easily we can fall into the trap I just described as "other people's" behavior. Heaven knows I do it myself.

I think it's just a normal, human habit, and one would be a saint if one never did it. We can become aware of it, though, and at least make an effort to stop focusing on the bad things we've experienced. All that does for us is make us miserable.

We might consider all the events in our lives, good and bad, as the movie or series of movies we've starred in. Like Rocky I, II and III, I've got Lee I, II, III and all the way up to however you make a Roman numeral 80, one for each year of my life. All in all they make a fine library of DVDs I can watch if I want. I'll always cherish them.

But I'd be pretty dumb if I spent much time watching them over and over. They're history. It doesn't much matter what's happened in my life so far; what matters is what happens now.

In a way I'm beginning a new movie right now, called Lee 81.

Not only do I get to star in it, I get to write and direct it. I'm the producer and the casting agent. I get to create this movie and the dozens that will follow any way I want! At least I have complete control over my own part, the lead. The rest of the cast will vary and will do all kinds of things that I don't expect.

Sometimes I'll get upset with them for behaving exactly opposite of how I wanted them to act because it means I have to change my whole plot. Here I'll have it all formulated in my mind and then one of the other leads will move or get married or pregnant or divorced, get mad at me, cheat me or be unexpectedly good to me. This crew will be uncontrollable, but what can you do?

I have a few options, as the director. I can yell and scream at them and try harder to get them to do what I want. I can try manipulating them, and goodness knows I have a lot of skills in that department. I can banish them from the set (my life) and look for new actors.

I can hate the whole process of making movies and become hostile and bitter and reclusive.

Or I can constantly re-write the script to accommodate the changes, keeping my lead reacting exactly the way I want. And I can either enjoy the process or be miserable; I get to decide even that.

So how do I want myself, the star, to be? It's grand to know I have the power to decide! I am in complete control of the star, regardless of any of the others' attitudes and behavior. Nobody in this whole world can change the way I choose to think and feel, no matter what they do, no matter how hard they may try to defeat me.

I am going to make movies that the entire audience will cheer about, because the only audience I have to appeal to is me, Lee. I can't lose! If I'm the writer, producer, director, star and audience I'll be a sure Oscar winner every year for the rest of my life.

I'll even be the camera person, and shoot exactly the shots I want to capture, which means I'll skip a lot of the unimportant stuff. I'll become an expert at changing the focus, exaggerating the shots that I want to enjoy and savor and maybe even shoot in slow motion so they last longer. I'll shoot the not-so-good events from a different angle, maybe focusing on one good detail, enlarging it to make it more important than the negative action that's going on in the background.

That focusing business is really essential if this movie is going to make me happy, and I'll practice that skill until I'm such a pro I'll be able to find the flower in any patch of weeds. Once I've found it I can make it stand out and look glorious, capturing its beauty so that the weeds around it are muted and hardly noticeable in its presence.

In that way I can truly be the master of my fate, the gifted creator of my destiny, absolutely and totally in charge of my beliefs, attitudes, feelings and behavior. I'll have tremendous power in my life.

Knowing that, I'll be free to stop trying to control the rest of the cast, too, which should make them a lot happier and easier to live with. If I can be happy in spite of their behavior or misbehavior there will be no more need to try to control them. How freeing that will be. Even if I think I know what's best for everybody (and of course I do!) I'll be able to let go of any need or desire to make them choose my recommendations. I'm free to tell them my ideas if I want to, but what they decide to do about them will no longer determine my happiness or unhappiness.

I did plenty of that in all the old movies and it somehow left me feeling worse rather than better, because I was always feeling responsible for others' lives. That's such an impossible position in which to be, I no longer even want to try.

Let them be responsible. I'm retiring from that thankless job. I can say honestly I gave it my best shot, though, for lo these many years, and my family will attest to that. I talked myself blue in the face for hours on end, trying to get this one and that one to see the light. Somehow I always felt if I explained it long enough and hard enough they'd come to see it "right." (My way, of course.) But do you think they did? Heck, no.

I'd be crazy to want to continue that behavior. It doesn't take me long to know when I'm licked, only 80-some years.

Since I'm producing my own movie, I can decide whether I want it to be a happy one or a tragedy. Maybe I want bits of both. But I know I want it to have a happy ending—and I want it to have lots of happiness all throughout!

Joy. Pleasure. Bliss. Fun. Happiness. Delight. Ecstasy. Elation. Cheer. Gladness. Exhilaration. Merriment. Recreation. Capers. Amusement. Romps. Frolic. Satisfaction. Play. Gratification. Feasts. Parties. Celebration. Games. Festivity. Appreciation. Revelry. Jubilation. Rejoicing. Gaiety. Diversion. What great words!

Little Orphan Annie used to say, "It makes me feel glad all over!"

Wouldn't it be fun to feel that way? To be able to savor life and relish each hour? To wake up in the morning feeling enthusiasm and eagerness, liking the day even before it gets off the ground?

Is all of that possible?

Probably not. At least no one I know experiences life that way. My guess is that it's more typical to wake up in the morning with a groan, of sorts, even if it's a silent one.

Many of us instantly find our heads filled with remembering the tasks and problems that face us that day, and our morning is off to a grim process of going about the business of enduring the procedure.

Somehow we manage. We swing our reluctant bodies out of bed and begin the battle of coping with life. Often we start with a stiff belt of coffee, sometimes accompanied by something sugary to help our minds find temporary strength. We may find some pleasure in a good, hot shower, and by the time we finish our daily rituals of lotioning, deodorizing, blowing dry, styling, and dressing we might even face the day with some enthusiasm.

But would we say we're feeling joy and gladness and all those other nifty words above? Most of us would not. Certainly there's a wide spectrum between unbounded exhilaration and utter despair. I choose not to agree with Thoreau, who speculated that "Most men live lives of quiet desperation." The vast majority of us manage to strike a balance that ranges from pretty darned happy to downright miserable, but we slide up and down the scale all the time.

Happiness has a different meaning to each one of us.

I've often thought Heaven must look exactly like South Coast Plaza in Costa Mesa, California. It's the most splendid mall I've ever seen, and my feelings there are all of those words above and then some. I can spend an entire day reveling in pure bliss, finally dragging my bags to the car in a state of utter exhaustion, and the feeling in my heart is a filled-to-the-brim, "That's how life should be!"

My friend Hope shakes her head in puzzled disbelief, however, and ponders how anything so dreadful to her can be so uplifting to me. She finds her happiest moments near the water. Born and raised in the Arizona desert, I'm not that drawn to the beach. (People here say, in fact, "Arizona is full of beaches; there's just no water by them.")

When I drive back to Winslow, my home town, I feel a deep stirring as I see the vast, sweeping vistas of flat,

flat land stretching for hundreds of miles with no trees in sight. A few red rocks add interest, and the deep red color of the land contrasts with the bluest sky in the whole world. To me that's God's country! Off in the distance are the buttes of the Painted Desert and the Petrified Forest, and Indian reservations are close around.

When we've taken friends there, however, they stare in absolute horror. "You lived here?" they gasp. "You like this?" Yep. But I can understand how grimly barren it looks to anyone who grew up where there are trees and flowers and mountains and water. Beauty is in the eye of the beholder for sure.

All pleasure is, of course. And we're so lucky when we know what brings us pleasure and can find it in our lives at least some of the time.

Most of us know exactly what kind of country we enjoy the most. And we know what activities are rewarding to us and which are distasteful. We know what kinds of people we like and those we probably wouldn't seek out as dinner partners.

And yet, in spite of our best efforts, often we can't describe ourselves as truly happy. What would it take to change our fair-to-middling mediocre states to delighted-fun-happiness states? Are we capable of making that happen? Or is it a myth or dream left from our childhood fairy-tale years that we must forego once and for all now that we're responsible adults?

Maybe we are enjoying life and we don't know it. Maybe happiness is simply the absence of unhappiness. Since we're not miserable, we think, might this be as good as it gets?

No way. As long as we're alive and breathing we can change the state we're in to a better, more fulfilling one. Even if we're content with our lives we can become more content. We have an endless capacity to improve our minds and our bodies and our spirits, and it can be an enjoyable lifelong project making those changes.

Sometimes it's helpful to think of our childhood.

To this day catching a whiff of pepper trees takes me back to the school I attended in sixth grade, and I'm filled with nostalgia. I can hear the sounds of children in the playground and taste the milk we were given at recess. The milk was never cold enough, but we drank it dutifully and hurried on to the relay races, which Eleanor Melendez always won. There was a boy named Morris Belakoff who had a crush on me, and since his father managed a dime store Morris gave me a 25-cent diamond ring which I still have, even though I didn't share his romantic feelings at the time.

Letting myself reminisce about that era brings on a host of memories that reminds me I was happy in those days. It was during World War Two, and we had a wonderful spirit of patriotism that united us and made us feel like were important. We bought savings stamps at school, learned all the armed forces songs, and planned to join the WACS or WAVES the minute we were old enough.

There were so many good things about being a child then, and all of it rushes back at the scent of a pepper tree.

Songs do it, too. Don't you love listening to the radio and hearing some music that takes you back to high school?

Suddenly you're caught up in a warm, delicious memory of the boy or girl you loved so much you thought you couldn't stand it. Maybe you can picture yourself dancing in the school gym and see all the streamers and decorations that transformed it into the grandest ballroom. You can still smell the gardenias that abounded on the girls' pastel formals made out of tulle and the carnations on their boyfriends' lapels. What marvelous, heady feelings we had then, tasting the beginnings of romantic attachments which we knew no mere parent had ever experienced. The band played whatever music was "the only kind there was" in those days, and we scoffed at any songs previous generations had enjoyed.

Hearing one of those tunes now can magically transport us back to the days of intense feelings which ran the gamut from absolute exhilaration all the way to total despair. It certainly wasn't all great.

And yet, looking back at it, it's easy to think those were rare, golden times that filled us with joy and pleasure.

Some of my male friends glow when they talk about making the touchdown that won the game. "I fell over that goal line, and it was the best day I ever had," says Gregg. "Nothing nowadays matches the thrill of that experience."

We don't forget the unpleasant events of our lives, but fortunately time has a way of softening them. And with the help of that time filter we can often see the larger picture: one of quality life overall that may have eluded us back when those incidents were occurring.

Perhaps we're like moths who, when they fly freely from their larvae stages, can look down and see the rich beauty of the Persian rug in which they used to dwell. When they were down there they could see nothing but the tall fibers of wool that imprisoned them, and only by growing up are they able to realize the splendid colors from which they emerged.

Still, the "picture albums" in our heads include plenty of good shots and lots of not-so-good ones. If we look at those albums we can often identify the best times we've had as well as the worst.

What was one of the times that you were your happiest? Not just an isolated recollection, but a period of weeks or months or maybe even years. Some people might answer, "Being a child when we lived in Iowa" or "When Dad was still living" or "Spending summers at my grandparents' farm."

Others find very little that was attractive about being a child, and their happiest times began when they were sent off to college or went into the service.

Men commonly recall with great affection their days in the armed forces. It seems the friends they made there were often extremely close, and the many bad experiences they shared only created deeper bonds between them. They can shake with laughter recalling the night Bob eluded the MPs' search, or the sergeant's face when….

At the time it may have been pure stress, but in retrospect the period had its share of real joy. Some remember it now as one of the best eras they ever lived through because of the growth they experienced as well as the friendships.

Many of us go back to our first jobs and the thrill of actually getting paychecks and feeling grown up. Tasting the adult world was usually a heady experience for each of us.

What were the qualities that made those such good times? It's interesting to dissect those passages in life, looking for exactly what made them appealing. Was it freedom that we felt? Knowing we were at least beginning to move away from the restraints our parents had placed on us felt good. Perhaps it was taking responsibility that filled us with pride, realizing we were trusted with specific tasks that someone knew we could handle.

Sometimes it was just the opposite atmosphere that we look back at as a golden time. Maybe you were happiest when you were idle. Perhaps you reflect now on long, lazy summer days when school was out and you didn't yet have a job. You slept late, hung out with your friends, went swimming or read one book after another, week after week. Was it the lack of responsibility that made you happy?

Being happy means something different for each one of us, and often we've never stopped to figure out what set of circumstances defines that state.

Looking back, were you happiest when you were deliciously idle? Importantly responsible? Productive? Creative? Physically involved or at rest? Alone or with others? With only one other person or with several?

Certainly you might have been happy in several of those situations, maybe even all of them.

As you peruse your early years you can discover the kinds of things that made you happiest and see if your life today gives you opportunities for similar experiences. Sometimes I ask a depressed client, "What did you like to do when you were in high school?"

One woman smiled dreamily and answered, "Go on dates, but my husband won't let me do that now."

You may have to spend some days or weeks considering this question, but inevitably you'll be able to find some activities that used to be pleasurable to you. Were you into team sports? Art? Music? Reading? Games? Going to movies? Did you enjoy hiking or practicing your golf swing? Long phone conversations with a close friend? Writing letters or short stories? Have you always thought it would be fun to write a book? What kind—romance, mystery, science fiction, adventure? Did you enjoy learning? Would you get a kick out of taking Spanish now, or French? How about a tap dance class or one in karate?

A friend of ours used to want to tend bar, but he's now a very successful attorney. He's considering taking a class in bartending just for fun.

Another friend who is a contractor is learning handwriting analysis.

Our opportunities for change and growth are endless. The only thing stopping us from pursuing them is us. And that's understandable, because we have pretty full lives already. On the other hand, if we want to get happier we have a plethora of choices to consider.

Of course, maybe your life is too full. Perhaps you're already working full-time and playing the rest of the time. Maybe you're over-extended, and your key to pleasure is eliminating some activities. To spend an entire weekend sleeping and reading might be just what you need.

Isn't it grand that you get to decide what you hanker for and then be able to go for it?

seven

Dependencies and Beliefs

As directors and stars of our own movies, we're constantly faced with a variety of decisions about how to make our production turn out the way we'd like. There are numerous skills that all the best directors use, and the more of these skills we can master, the better our movies will be.

One of the hardest tasks we face in life is letting go. We're asked, from time to time, to let go of those we love, to let go of certain responsibilities, of traditions that have meant the world to us, of expectations that we've held since childhood, of beliefs that seem no longer to be true. And that's just a partial list.

People tell us letting go is necessary, and that it will make us happier. Are we supposed to believe them? Even when it feels like we're abandoning someone we love, or giving up a principle for which we might have fought to the death?

Probably so.

The very things we want to cling to so tightly are often the ones that we have to release for our own good as well as for those around us. Many times that "holding on" is the source of our pain, and we discover after the fact that giving it up has indeed made us feel better. But it sure doesn't seem like that at the time. So we hang on tooth and nail, gritting our teeth in determination, giving everything that's in us to the effort of holding on.

Sometimes we feel sheer terror at the thought of the change we'd face if we couldn't hold on any longer, and it seems so frightening we tighten our grip even more.

Someone pointed out that newborn babies' hands are clenched into tiny fists, and it takes them much of their lives to learn to relax and let things go. By the time people die in old age their hands are open. I don't know if that's literally true, but symbolically it is. In the process of living we try so hard to get, to accumulate, to save; buying things to please us, holding onto the people we love and to our responsibilities. But gradually our hands are opening more and more, and finally we discover we've gotten pretty good at letting go! That's when life becomes its most pleasurable.

There are many facets of holding on, and one of them is the habit of dependency. The term "co-dependency" became a buzz word many years ago, and many of us define ourselves that way. Co-dependency is an addiction to a relationship that seems to be love but is actually unwholesome. Loving someone more than ourselves or at the expense of our own good is an addiction, a substitute for love. My belief is that, co-dependent or not, dependency of any kind is usually crippling in some way. Yet our human nature is often to seek out someone on whom to depend. Once we find them we glom onto them, which may reduce both of us to unhappy shadows of the people we could be.

Frequently we feel like we're independent because we're self-sufficient in seemingly every way. We may be physically and emotionally strong, financially secure, grounded firmly in our spirituality, and yet miserably dependent on certain "rules" for living. Even relatively insignificant beliefs like "Dinner dishes should always be done immediately following dinner" can make us dependent.

One of my clients complains that she and her husband have an arrangement in which she cooks and he cleans up. "But," she wails, "he wants to leave the dishes until morning, and I can't stand that. We fight about it every night."

She is dependent on seeing her belief carried out. When that belief is disregarded she feels very threatened. Having the kitchen restored to neatness is one of my preferences, as well, but if it comes to a choice of having someone else do it in the morning or doing it myself, I'll give up my preference in a second. Naturally she has the option of doing the dishes herself at whatever hour she chooses, but that wouldn't solve the problem. She'd still feel resentful because the work load wasn't even.

Her husband handles the money—all the money. Both of them are professional people earning some fifty thousand a year apiece. But it is his firm belief that she "couldn't" handle paying the bills, balancing the checking account, etc. With her giving him her paycheck to manage, he feels a sense of control over their finances, and he's comfortable. Not surprisingly she resents his implication that she's less capable than he, and also angry that she has little say over how her money is spent. They fight over that issue long and hard.

The poor man paled when I suggested making changes, and his response was so strong it showed a dependency. He believes he needs to be the one in charge of money, and it would be catastrophic if he weren't. He depends on that happening for his peace of mind.

It's no different from her depending on having the kitchen cleaned up in the evening instead of the morning. Both of them believe strongly that "one does things this way, and any other way is wrong." The level of the discomfort they feel at the thought of change indicates their degree of dependency.

All of us have some dependency on beliefs. The belief that women shouldn't vote was widely held in the early 1900s. Many men felt threatened at letting it go. To the extent that it bothered them, they were dependent.

I'm dependent on a lot of dumb ideas. One used to be that my birthday should be duly noted by all who love me. Like Liz Taylor celebrating her sixtieth in Disneyland with much pomp and ceremony, I'd like nationwide coverage. My preference for the day would be marching bands, parties, gifts, food, revelry and fireworks. Even then I'd probably go to bed feeling, "Is that all there is?"

My family knows this, and they very graciously sing to me and give me presents and take me out to restaurants, all of which I deeply appreciate. They're honoring my dependency. If they ignored it I would be sad, so that's how I know it's a dependency.

Is it wrong to be dependent on ideas or beliefs? Of course not. But we need to recognize them as dependencies rather than God's Rules Chiseled In Stone, and also know that our vulnerability increases with the number of dependencies we allow ourselves to have.

If I depend on life to be fair I'm going to be disappointed a lot. Depending on drivers to drive safely doesn't assure that they will. Depending on politicians to be honest and open is clearly an old-fashioned belief, and if I cling to that I'll be disillusioned over and over again. I can't even depend on all religious leaders to be truthful.

And yet I find myself depending on all of the above and feeling disappointed and sad when I learn things didn't measure up to my expectations.

But if that's true, how are we supposed to live our lives? We can't not depend on things just to avoid feeling let down. Actually we have to depend on certain facts to be able to structure our lives. At the same time, though, it would help us to remember the old saw about depending on nothing but death and taxes. Otherwise our expectations will be disappointed constantly, and our unhappiness will be in direct proportion to the number of beliefs we cling to fiercely.

What I'd like to achieve is the awareness that I can expect certain behavior from people, and at the same time know it's not assured. And that I can stand it when things don't work out like I had pictured.

I'd like to walk through life with a small level of expectancy, and a huge amount of flexibility, allowing for all the times my beliefs will have to change.

Of course sticking to a belief can be a noble thing to do, especially if I work toward making some kind of positive change for the good of mankind. Had women simply accepted being barred from voting, nothing would have changed. If we blindly and blandly allowed life to happen without trying to spot and effect changes that would benefit society, we'd miss the opportunity to contribute. Certainly we want to improve the quality of life on earth as much as we can.

But to feel dependent on that happening is what brings us the pain. Perhaps there are causes where it's worth some discomfort. In those cases we need to pursue our goals with courage and determination, undaunted by the difficulties. But we can't expect it to be stress-free. We can work toward effecting changes without depending on their happening in a certain time line.

To the extent that we can let go of our emotional neediness, we'll enjoy life as we work. You'd think that by knowing that and believing it so strongly, I'd able to let go of every belief that causes me trouble in life. (I wish!) But I struggle mightily to let go of some really unimportant and yet deeply held beliefs that cause me pain.

One is the conviction that everybody needs a good night's sleep. While it's enormously important to me (the world is either good or bad depending on how I slept the night before), to my children it's no big deal. Needless to say I became much more comfortable when they grew up and moved out and I no longer knew how much they slept. But when one of them visits and his flight arrives near midnight I plunge headlong into my old worry mode. Morning finds me tippy-toeing around and sh-sh-ing everyone in the house because our son needs his sleep. He is unconcerned and seems to awake refreshed regardless of the number of hours he slept. When I think of the hours I've wasted agonizing over my kids' sleeping habits, I determine to let go of that silly obsession I have.

So far I've made just a smidgen of progress. I've a long, long way to go. The word "obsession," then, is really another word for dependency. I depend on my people to get my recommended amount of sleep in order for me to be happy. And I'm fighting a losing battle. I must let go of it for my peace of mind—and everyone else's, for that matter. It doesn't endear me to my children, although they tolerate my concern with fond amusement as they ignore it.

Why is it so hard to let go? Because in our early years of life we formed our beliefs of how life should be. We looked around us and drew conclusions about what made life good and what made it bad. We were determining way back then that "Life is a place where…"

Every belief we have stems from incidents we experienced or observed years ago, and most of those are so strongly rooted in us that letting go of them is like ripping out our hearts. We've all tried to pull up weeds that refused to budge. We have to dig them out or soak them deeply to get them out of our garden.

Letting go of our beliefs, even the ones that cause us pain, takes a lot of deep soaking and digging. We have to be really convinced all that effort is going to enhance our lives, or we're not going to do it. "Letting go" sounds easy if we picture letting go of a balloon. But it's more like "losing weight," which isn't nearly as easy as losing an earring. You have to work hard to get rid of it. The end result of your labors, however, is the ecstasy of freedom.

It might be helpful to list the things we'd like to let go of or release. Many of them are just under the surface of our awareness, and bringing them up to the surface helps us deal with them. There's something therapeutic about making a list says, "There. I've written it down. That shows I've acknowledged it, I'm facing it, and I'm on the way to dealing with it."

Sometimes the very act of writing it makes us remember it even if we don't refer to the list. Often I've made a grocery list and forgotten it at home when I go to the market. I'm always impressed with how many of the items I remember to buy because I can visualize much of what I wrote down. Writing it on paper sort of writes it in our minds.

So jotting down items I want to let go of is a good beginning in taking charge of the niggling nuisance traits we let bother us. My list would include some of the following:

Feeling responsible for my children's happiness.
Thinking I need to solve everyone's problems.
My expectation that Larry should think like I do.
My fear of disapproval.

That's all I can think of at the moment, and it's quite enough. I know others will pop into my mind from time to time, and I can add them as they do. There's no need to sit and compose a complete list all at once, because we can't let go of all the items immediately anyway. There's no rush. It's better to be casual about it, looking at it as an entertaining exercise we're choosing to do.

Frequently we scare ourselves to death by determining we're going to change a habit, and we set about doing it so grimly we begin to feel punished. Pretty soon we feel so sorry for the way we're treating ourselves, we give up the whole idea.

If we can remain gentle with ourselves, like a kindly grandmother or grandfather, we stand a better chance of doing what we set out to do. In case you, like I, didn't have a kind grandparent, you just make one up. Imagine what the ideal grandparent would have been like and treat yourself that way as you progress.

Even the language we use with ourselves is important—it's either encouraging or discouraging. Ideally we'd encourage ourselves (and others) all the time, but typically we're too quick to jump on the mistakes.

We make life twice as hard by stewing about a specific problem and then compounding it by beating ourselves up over it. For example:

This Friday we're having the meeting of the Adlerian Society of Arizona at our home. This is a group composed mostly of counselors and educators who share a belief in the teachings of the late psychiatrist Alfred Adler. It's a wonderful bunch of people…the nicest, friendliest, most accepting folks you could find. We're fond of quoting Adler's "Have the courage to be imperfect," an encouraging thought if there ever was one. We believe it, we preach it, and we live it.

Except when we're meeting at my house. Then, as the date grows closer, I begin to feel as if I need to be perfect after all. "Company is coming!" a voice deep within me cries. "Time to spiff up the house, the yard, wash the windows, buy lots of food, and lose five pounds!"

Last night there was a message on the answering machine reminding me of the meeting, so it was on my mind when I went to bed. Guess what I did: I began to feel anxious. I thought all the thoughts in the last paragraph and then began to wish Larry would do more to help me. The fact that he'd agreed to help on Friday afternoon didn't seem to reassure me. So I alternated between picturing the tasks that awaited me and resenting Larry for not helping more the last time the group met here.

Then I dreamed that the people came and there was not a speck of food in the house. (I've had that dream a hundred times, and in it I'm helpless, embarrassed, and thoroughly miserable.)

This morning when I woke it made me smile at myself, and at how quickly I can fall back into bad patterns I thought I'd licked. I realize now that the whole episode reflected three of the four traits I want to let go of. They are:

Thinking I need to solve everyone's problems (by having available the exact foods and drinks each person likes).

My expectations that Larry should think like I do. (Then he would do everything I think is necessary, and he would love doing it!)

My fear of others' disapproval (in thinking I must wash the windows, etc., lest they think I'm a filthy slob).

So, okay, that's interesting to realize, but now what I must not do is get angry with myself for still having those thoughts. I complicate the issue if I beat myself up further. In the past I would have chastised myself harshly for holding on to those tendencies. My thinking would have been, "You stupe! How can you still worry about all those things, knowing what you do? When the heck are you going to stop trying to measure up to everybody's expectations, which they probably don't have, anyway? I can't believe you're still trying to be perfect, trying to give the impression of being an immaculate housekeeper!" And so on.

It feels really good to recognize that I've made progress in that area; that I'm not nearly so hard on myself as I used to be.

Because there's no rush. I have my whole life in which to play around with this behavior, and I realize I like the concept of "play" way more than the idea of having to "work" on it. (Work can be fun too, of course, so use whichever word you feel like using.) The idea is that the process of change can take as long as it needs to take, and our self-worth needn't depend on the speed at which we lick our problems. Besides, it seems like there are always new problems to replace the old ones anyway, right? We're never going to have the perfect life.

Still, slowly changing some of the behavior that gets on our nerves makes us feel good and so is worth doing. Writing down four of the traits I want to let go of was enlightening to me, and I know I'll find myself identifying them often as I repeat the mistakes. In fact I might number them. To be able to identify the behavior so effortlessly might make it a little less serious and formidable. Those four action categories would become like familiar friends whom I recognize and acknowledge when I see them. Instead of being frustrating enemies who continue to defeat me, they could evolve into little customs that are more endearing than dangerous.

"Oops, there's number three," I could think with a smile. Kind of like a little five-year-old neighbor who used to live next door. The minute one of us went out to get the mail or go to our car this boy would appear, eager to chat. He was such a cute little guy you couldn't get upset with him, and yet he'd have taken all our time if we'd let him. We got good at tossing him friendly hellos and beating hasty retreats. If we were pulling weeds and had to pass the time anyway we'd welcome his company.

But we were in control; he wasn't. We can become so familiar with the habits we're dealing with we'll see them with the same cavalier attitude: an amused recognition, but not something that's going to control our lives. Rather the knowledge that, like the little kid next door, it's going to continue trying to involve us. But we can either spend time entertaining it or walk away from it; it's our decision.

The little kid eventually grew up a bit and had no further interest in us. He found friends and interests of his own. Our little annoying habits will distance themselves from us, too; it's a guarantee. The more we stop giving them our time and energy, the less they hang around.

And using the balloon image is one way we can stop giving them our time and energy. We can just let them go.

Last night Larry and I were discussing something that one of his friends was doing. I disagreed with the advice Larry had given him, and made my point a couple of times. Larry continued defending his stance, and suddenly I remembered: I want to let go of my expectation that Larry should think and feel exactly like I do.

So I thought to myself, "Just let it go," and the image of releasing the balloon flashed in my mind. It was so easy! I smiled at myself, enjoying the awareness that I didn't have to convince him of anything. What his friend did was his business, and the same was true of Larry.

What a relief it was not to feel like Larry should think like I do, and isn't it dumb that I ever think he should! Of course rationally, logically, I would always have said he needn't think like I do, but something within me has always wished he would. It was a rewarding baby step of progress to know I could let that expectation go.

Some expectations will be easier to let go of than others. But there's no deadline. Whenever we find ourselves able to let go of any expectation, we'll be rewarded with a happier state of mind.

eight

Co-Stars and Friends

One of the most important parts of the movie you star in is the cast and crew. Without them, the movie wouldn't ever make it to the theater! And when you watch the videos of your life, it's always enjoyable to see your friends on the screen.

Friends, in fact, are an important part of life.

"When I met a man who told me he had no friends I thought to myself, 'Steer clear of this guy,'" Ruth said. "You know there's something wrong with a person like that."

I hadn't thought of friendship as a criterion for judging people until Ruth made that observation, but after thinking about it I'm coming to understand her thinking. "Something wrong" is a pretty loose description, of course, but possibly a reasonable aid in judging people with whom we're considering a relationship.

There could, of course, be many reasons for finding oneself in the unlikely position of having no friends, and there could certainly be exceptions to Ruth's rule. But by and large friends are as much a part of our lives as are food and shelter, and it's difficult to imagine a situation in which we would have none.

Sometimes it's a temporary state, like when we've moved to a new city and know no one. It's part of the stress of a move, in fact, that lack of a support system; and often we fill the gap by calling family and friends out of town. Hopefully we can begin quickly to make new friends, usually at our work place and/or our apartment complex or neighborhood.

The making of a new friend often has a feeling of pleased excitement connected with it. Some vibe usually has to be present in order for us to think of someone as a potential friend, because many of the folks we encounter we don't even consider trying to build a friendship with. We rule them out on an unconscious level.

Those who pass the first unconscious test have exhibited some quality that appeals to us, often without our even being specifically aware of it. If we get to spend enough time with a person we may find several qualities we like in them, and if they're finding some in us, we may both feel the pleasure of a friendship developing.

Sometimes they develop quickly. Other times it takes a while. Sometimes we know almost at once what the prognosis is, and yet occasionally we find ourselves wrong. Have you ever had an encounter with a stranger who seemed so unpleasant that you never, ever would have guessed you'd end up liking the person, and yet you have?

At times it takes many encounters before we begin to change our first impressions. For me the change comes more easily when I know how that person thinks and feels. The more openly he reveals his thoughts, the faster I come to understand him. Understanding is almost sure to lead to positive feelings in me, and I want to learn more.

When folks are closed and guarded I find it difficult to feel enthusiastic about them, because I flat can't get to know them!

That's why I almost always come to genuinely like the clients I see. The more intimately we discuss how it feels to be inside this person's head, the more I can relate to them. I discover commonality in practically everybody. It still amazes me how much alike we all seem to be once we get past the superficial differences. And the more we have in common, the better our chances for deepening our friendship.

I've discovered that's true in reverse as well. When I have the courage to open up to an acquaintance and let her see inside my mind, she usually can relate to me and accept me. That gives her more courage to share feelings and thoughts with me, and that's what friendship is all about. To me. It's different with some people, I know, especially with many men.

While women tend to have friends with whom they share their innermost selves, men often have friends with whom they simply share activities. A man might have his golf friends, his hiking friends, his poker friends and his job friends. A woman is more likely to count her friends as the ones to whom she "can tell anything."

So I guess it's up to each one of us to figure out for what purpose we want friends at all. Any reason is a good one, and there are almost no bad ones. I say "almost" because some people want only "friends" they can use. And then, in my estimation, they're really not seeking friends but rather objects designed for their specific wants.

An example of that from my own life is a feeling of disappointment I've gotten occasionally when I've thought "Janet" and I were becoming friends. Let's say we seemed to have genuine respect and regard for one another and some things in common. So we've moved on to the next step of developing a friendship, making plans to get together. We agree to have lunch.

I'm eager to get to know Janet better over this lunch, and happy when she starts telling me what's going on in her life. I'm genuinely interested. I listen, I comment, I nod, and Janet talks on. By the time the waitress brings the check I realize I realize that the "conversation" is really a monologue.

I haven't gotten to tell her anything about my life, and I want to do that some, too. I wait for a pause (sometimes a long time coming) and then I mention something about what's going on with me. Janet looks at her watch and says, "My goodness, look at the time! I've got to run. But this has been a great lunch, and I'd like to do it again soon."

I feel a cloud over my head, and I think, "She doesn't want me as a friend after all; she simply wants an audience."

Now I have some choices. I can smile falsely (my friend Tom calls that a "smile") and say, "Wasn't it fun! I'll call you," and resolve not to pursue this friendship anymore.

I could become more competitive, and the next time we meet I could jump in first with tales of my own, and talk faster and faster and never pause for breath so she can't get a word in. But I'd hate that.

What I've taken to doing is sharing my feelings with her during that first lunch. I say something like, "I enjoy hearing about your kids and everything, and I want to tell you some of the things I've been experiencing too." Sometimes the Janet might say, "Oh sure. Tell me."

But I can tell when she looks preoccupied that she really doesn't want to hear.

Maybe if I were an aggressive person I would jump in and so would she and we would both enjoy ourselves. It may be because I am not an aggressive person that I wait respectfully for a "turn."

So I'm not saying the Janets of the world are wrong and I'm the good guy. We just have different styles.

I've learned that I most enjoy people whose standards for communicating are similar to my own. My closest friends are those who innately take turns. There's a nearly equal amount of give and take between us. Those are the friends I call the most often.

That doesn't mean I don't enjoy running into the Janets at parties or in the mall. I can truly delight in seeing them again and spending a few minutes hearing their latest recitations. I can enjoy them, but they probably won't become my good friends.

What are friends for? Can we get by in this life without them? Of course we can, but our lives would be sadly lacking. We can get by without our legs, too, or our eyes, and being without friends would be even more difficult to most of us.

Friends serve many purposes, and we can't expect one friend to fill all our social needs. But all our friends put together form one of the three things Alfred Adler prescribed as necessary for us to have happiness:

Work. A love-sex relationship. And friends.

Ideally we'd have all three, Adler believed. Most of us have the drive to pursue those three areas in our lives, but sometimes we take the "friends" part much more for granted than the other two.

Certainly we look for a marriage or relationship partner, and most of us know we must work, but we often see friends as simply "there," helping us pass time. We don't really recognize how valuable they are to us.

Valuable, yes, but not ever maintenance-free. Like everything worthwhile in life, friends take some effort on our parts. To have a friend we have to be one, and that means making sure we keep in touch. Sometimes the contact can't be very often because of distance and/or available time, but the relationship will be about as deep as the energy we put into keeping it alive.

As we get older we seem to be less willing to put forth as much effort as we did when we were young. Children instinctively reach out to one another, innately recognizing how they enhance each other's lives. In grade school most of us had dozens of friends we actively played with. Junior high became tougher largely because we were so self conscious and insecure we found it difficult to interact with our schoolmates, who were every bit as troubled and unsure of their social worth. High school became smoother, by and large, although often we limited our friends to one or two or three close ones. Even so we felt comfortable with our classmates, and developed a camaraderie in each class. Joanne was my "history friend." Annette and I walked to school together. Marion and I chatted during art class.

Though not always "soul mates," we kept each other supported by sharing experiences on a daily basis, and it was easy. We were one another's captive audience simply because everybody had to go to school.

The friends we made as youngsters were often the closest in our entire lives. Our worlds revolved around each other. We learned so much from one other, and felt our self-esteem rise and fall as our sometimes rocky friendships thrived and struggled. All of those relationships were helping us learn how to handle our grownup ones, including marriage.

If we were lucky we continued interacting with friends through college and/or first jobs. Our friends were the most important part of our lives in those days.

But many of us began to cut down on the hours spent with friends as we grew older and took on more responsibilities. Perhaps after we got married, we tried to fill all our needs with just our spouses. Often we say, "My husband/wife is my best friend." That's wonderful! But we're cheating ourselves if we drop all the others, because no one person can possibly fill the shoes of the many friends we enjoyed when we put more time into them.

Many women, more than men, thought of girl friends as pals who helped pass the time till we found our men. With amazing naïveté we thought those men were going to make us happy all by themselves. In my book on marriage, <u>I Do? (Being Happy Being Married)</u>, I address that mistaken belief at great length. After we've been married a while we realize how differently men and women think and relate, and sometimes it's only then that we come to truly appreciate and cherish the friendships we have with people of our own sex.

Sometimes we can feel more completely understood by a girl friend than we ever can by our husbands. Men and women are wired so differently that it's difficult to get inside each others' heads and know how the other feels when we've never experienced some of the same problems.

What do we want from our friends? And what can we give them? I think it varies, each friendship filling a different role in our lives. With one, our common denominator might be the work we do. With another it might be our homes or our neighborhood. Discussing men and husbands seems to be pretty popular with almost all my friends. So is food. Many women think about food much of the time, and I'm one of them, so I love finding people who share that consuming (no pun intended) interest!

Another friend goes to plays and movies a lot, and that becomes a common topic between us. And I'm thrilled to have a walking friend, with whom I can walk two and a half miles each day while sharing thoughts and feelings as well.

Long ago I read that we each need a friend who's richer than we are, as well as one who's poorer. We should have one smarter and one dumber, one better-looking and one worse-looking. That way we keep our perspective, the article explained. I remember reading it aloud to my mother-in-law, who giggled and said, "I think that's why my friend Gail likes me; I'm her friend who's poorer, dumber and uglier."

Who knows what makes us attracted to one another? Sometimes we're not even sure ourselves. But when the chemistry is there we know it. Our friend Randall says, "We go through life searching for members of our tribe." It does seem as if we're seeking a particular kind of individual who complements some deep part of ourselves.

A musician I know laughs as he recounts stories of the various bands he played drums with during World War Two. He says the guys had such great times together and made such terrific music they were always saying, "After the war we'll have to get together!" They never did. But I believe their intentions, because I've had that thought so many times myself. "Let's not lose touch after graduation." "Just because you're moving out of state, we mustn't let our friendship go." "Write!"

But more often the friendship does go, and maybe that's okay. We probably wouldn't have enough hours in the day to maintain all the friendships we've thought we'd continue. Sometimes it's time to move on.

Another factor is change, because each of us is always doing that. We realize somewhere along the way that what we had in common with a certain person is no longer important to us.

When I was in my early thirties and heading toward a depression I had a good friend I'll call Marge. She and I would call each other every day and complain to one another. We whined about our husbands, about how hard we worked, how many miles we had to drive our kids every day, and about the cost of medical bills. We whimpered about the whole world. Nothing was right, nobody understood us, and life just wasn't worth a plugged nickel.

After I got some counseling I began to get un-depressed, and life began to change dramatically for me. Marge remained the same as she'd always been. I came to dread her phone calls, they were such downers, but I felt sorry for her so I continued the friendship for a couple more years. Finally I had the good sense to realize we had almost nothing in common anymore, and whatever interest I'd had in being her friend was long gone. I stopped calling, with some feelings of guilt.

I know now the guilt was unnecessary. There was a bit of grandiosity in me to think my phone calls meant that much to Marge, and to assume that she needed me in her life. She found other friends, of course, who were thinking like she was, and I found some on my wavelength. When friends lose commonality, they grow apart.

Sometimes people don't feel equally interested in each other from the start. I've known both men and women that I'd love to develop close friendships with, but I could tell after my attempts in that direction that they couldn't have been less interested. "Why?" I'd ask myself. "Why doesn't Janie like me when I like her so much?"

Who knows? I wasn't "a member of her tribe," probably.

It would be foolish to waste much time regretting those missed friendships when there are so many potential ones available out there. We never need to be lonely if we take the responsibility for seeking friends.

They can't all be best friends, for those are scarce as hen's teeth. It's said we're lucky to have five dear, close buddies, and I would agree with that. Even one or two of those are a blessing. But we can find dozens of friends who are perfectly acceptable. With enough time some of them may become the special friends.

What are the drawbacks of friends? The man Ruth steered clear of must have found them detrimental to his life. Why? My first guess is that his own self-esteem was not up to snuff. We can like other people only as much as (and no more than) we like ourselves. If, on a scale of one to a hundred, I like myself only a three, that's all I can like you. It stands to reason I'm certainly not going to want anyone who's worth only a three hanging around my life.

People in that predicament are truly tragic figures. Mingling with others teaches us so much and helps us grow. Change and growth help build our self-esteem. So we keep ourselves stuck in an impossible situation when we shut out friends. Our self-image becomes steadily worse as we notice all the sociability around us and feel more and more alienated. Man's greatest need is to belong, according to Adler, and the feeling of not belonging is close to despair.

A person who's chosen that direction has done it unconsciously, for the most part, in a misguided attempt to protect himself. He's probably been hurt way back in his childhood and formed the opinion that people can't be trusted. People are going to hurt you. That gets intertwined with his lack of self-worth. ("If I were any good, people would like me. They don't seem to, therefore I must be no good.") The first bricks of his protective wall probably went up before he was six years old.

Unfortunately people do hurt each other, although generally it's not intentional. The bumper sticker that says "Hell is other people" is partly right, in that they're the source of most of our pain. On the other hand, they're also the source of most of our pleasure, so "Heaven must be other people" too. One of our lifetime challenges is learning how to interact with them.

We can look at them in many ways, one being as "extras" in our movie. Extras just sit around movie sets waiting for their turn to mill about on the street or in the soda fountain or wherever the scene is being filmed. They have no importance in the story except to add credibility.

Their purpose is simply to enhance believability, to look good. Some folks like to surround themselves with "extras" because it makes them feel popular and sought after. They like having an entourage of people whom they view as accessories, improving their image the same way driving a Mercedes might.

Sometimes they spend a great deal of money entertaining this large group, and indeed it can pay off. People may tend to "court" them just to get invited to their parties. It's not a negative situation at all, because all the people are getting their needs met. They sip champagne and eat delicious foods, admire one another's clothes, and are all pleased to be included in this "cast of thousands." No harm done.

If the relationships are a bit shallow they're at least time-consuming in a positive way. Perhaps they're like chewing gum: not very nutritious but quite pleasant.

Some people seek acquaintances to advance their businesses: networking, it's called. There's nothing wrong with that either. It's more rewarding than paying for advertising, and sometimes an actual friendship develops as a result.

Some want companions to fill out bridge foursomes or tennis teams. Sports can't be played by oneself, after all.

There are those who get involved with others simply because they're pleasers who can't say "no." When their children go to school and they're invited to attend P.T.A. meetings they feel they should. When volunteers are requested to help with the school carnival they dutifully raise their hands. Not because they care a whit about the carnival, the school or the people, but because they hate disapproval.

They agree, often very pleasantly, to join other groups simply because they "can't say no."

John Bradshaw did a series on public TV called Homecoming in which he recommended we practice saying "No." First we say it to ourselves as we do housework or go driving or anytime we're alone. Aloud we say, "Nope. No way. Nosirree. Not a chance. No way, José. Count me out. Not gonna happen. No! No, no." Etc.

After we've gotten good at uttering the sounds we can practice on a real live person, like maybe a spouse or a real friend. We explain to them what we're attempting, and if they're willing to play, we respond negatively to everything they say or ask.

Finally we get to practice on legitimate favor-asking folk in the real world. I think it's a marvelous idea. It feels awfully good to be able to say "no" when that's what we want to say, and "yes" if that's how we feel. If we need lessons or classes on assertiveness training, we'd undoubtedly be glad we took them.

What we want to achieve is feeling comfortable enough around people to be able to be honest. Otherwise we either withdraw from them or punish them in some way. A good slogan is "Don't punish people, educate them."

We have to respect them enough to clue them in on our thinking. We have to risk honesty, even knowing it might cause an upset. Having the courage to share our thoughts, beliefs and feelings is the greatest gift we can give. And only then are we able to enjoy a true friendship, one in which we can support and be supported.

A circle of friends provides us with our very own "lab" in which to practice getting along with people. We're bound to make mistakes in dealing with each other, and hopefully we'll learn how to forgive.

In some families forgiveness doesn't occur. The rule taught by example is "Anyone who screws up is dead." The children watch their parents discard friends and neighbors one by one because of some disagreement, so of course they grow up thinking that's what one does.

Some even shut out their own family members for not measuring up. We all know brothers and sisters who refuse even to speak to each other.

The saddest thing is how they cheat themselves of the opportunity to learn and grow, when they could be experimenting in their labs on how to resolve problems and learn cooperation.

We walk around for years and years with unfinished business that continues to eat away at us, carrying old garbage about long-ago hurts, and yet we refuse to address them with the proper parties and seek resolution. Perhaps it's pride that makes us reluctant to try again.

By and large I attribute it to fear. We're afraid of getting hurt again, so we chum down our feelings, throw back our shoulders and march along through life like brave little soldiers. We act as if those old soured relationships don't bother us a bit. Who needs that old friend, anyway? And that one, too. Hey, I can get along just fine if I never see my cousin again, we say. And that goes for Aunt Lena, too. Ha! And I thought my friend Irma was different; I trusted her. Boy was I stupid. Never again, no sir. I don't trust anybody from here on out.

Pretty soon we may be dangerously close to becoming reclusive, choosing loneliness over the risk of more hurt.

Actually it does take courage to stay involved with people. We deserve to pat ourselves on the back if we have stayed involved, and we need be kind to ourselves if we haven't, because of the constant challenge it presents.

But is staying involved with people worth it? Oh, my, yes. A friend can be priceless. We get out of anything what we put into it, and pursuing relationships is well worth the cost.

After all, a movie with only one actor would be dull indeed.

nine

Enjoy the Music

Some of the best moments in movies owe their success to the music behind the scene. When you picture certain moments on the screen, often the music that accompanied them comes to mind as well.

All my life I have had some song—any song—running through my mind. So did my mother, and so does my son Lindsay. It's a family gift/curse.

The song changes frequently, and it's usually the last song I've heard, but it is with me every waking moment of every single day. A song I like is one thing, but many times I'll be singing one I don't like, and it goes on in my brain endlessly until finally I realize I'm hating it. I might spend an entire afternoon cleaning house to the tune of "Little Brown Jug" if that's what the ice cream truck was playing when it passed.

Fortunately, when I get sick of it I can make a decision literally to "change my tune," and go with that one for a while.

If I start a show tune I often continue through the whole Broadway musical, mentally hearing each tune in its proper order. Most of the time it's fine; it's cheap entertainment. But if I'm trying to fall asleep at night and I'm thinking of "Here Come the Jets" from West Side Story, I'll take every melody through to the movie's finale, "Somewhere"—a long process, especially in the middle of the night.

So I've learned to switch to the University of Arizona's alma mater if it's time to sleep; a sedate, stately and somehow soporific song much more conducive to slumber than "Officer Krupke."

Where does my tune go when I do sleep? It waits patiently. When I wake up to use the bathroom it jumps back to life for those few minutes, and then subsides till I awaken the next time, greeting me first thing in the morning.

Lindsay and I will sometimes ask one another "What are you singing?" and smile at sharing a moment of bonding and understanding. It's like two people who have been kidnapped by aliens in a flying saucer might feel, knowing few others probably have any idea what this dubious gift is like.

I do have a reason for telling about this peculiarity. Years ago I read an article in some psychology magazine that a man who with continuous music in his head had it removed through hypnosis and suddenly found himself facing horrible fears and memories from which his melodies had protected him.

I sought out my mentor, Father Bill McCartin, who taught me the importance of keeping apples in our barrels (read my <u>Nurturing Yourself and Others</u> book for an explanation). I explained my continual preoccupation with music, told him what the magazine had said, and asked if he thought I had some problem that needed uncovering.

He looked thoughtful for a few seconds, considering the question. Then he smiled reassuringly. "I certainly doubt it indicates anything deep and troubling," he said. "Music is very important to you. You say your mother always had a song, and Lindsay does. I can't think it signifies anything at all. If I were you I'd forget the article you read and just enjoy the music."

With that reassuring permission I accepted my mind-music completely and truly do enjoy it most of the time.

It would be too simplistic, however, to imply that because a certain person tells you "something is okay, just enjoy it," that you can rely on that advice. You still have to decide whether or not you agree with the message. I've received a lot of advice in my life, as you have, and much of it we discard immediately.

In the end only I am responsible for my decisions and my behavior. I can blame no one else if his or her advice doesn't work for me.

How do we know what to do? When is it a good idea to accept a trait or a habit and "just enjoy the music," and when should I try to get over it?

The trouble is there isn't a pat answer. It usually isn't a case of black or white, right or wrong, do this rather than that.

It's more like, "Well, in some cases this might be the best thing to do, but on the other hand it might not be." Sometimes it's a matter of trial and error. We have to go down one road for a while and see what happens, and if things get worse we backtrack and go down a different road. And there are generally many roads.

We might decide that for now we're going to accept something and live with it, and down the line we may reverse that decision and try again to change.

Science has learned that much of who we are is determined genetically. Physical appearance as well as mental capacity and personality are programmed into our DNA at the moment of conception, and many of those are with us for life. I can't make my brown eyes blue. But I can (and do) color my brown hair blonde.

If I have a tendency to chubbiness or skinniness I can fight it with diet and exercise, and I can usually achieve results in direct proportion to the amount of effort I'm willing to expend.

But I may not be able to be model thin without developing anorexia or bulimia, and we know that kind of behavior is destructive, even fatal.

That's when I might decide to accept my body type, rather than try to make myself into something that's virtually impossible. Still, ideally I'll continue to be self-disciplined and wise in my food and exercise choices to the best that I can healthily be.

Only I get to make that decision, since I am the producer of my own movie.

We have to/get to make a lot of decisions like that, and no one can make them for us, although a lot of people try. Truth be told, when someone tries to get me to change they're almost certainly going to fail. I change only when I want to change, and so do you.

Sometimes it takes us a while even to recognize what options we have, because we're so caught up in dealing with a particular circumstance that complicates things for us. We might complain about it, try to ignore it, even pray about it, and it might take us a long time to recognize the choices available to us.

Once we do, we may still be reluctant to make the choice. It may feel like too big a step to choose either course, because there's always a price tag. Changing to a behavior that's beneficial to us will usually have some difficulty attached to it, and normally we don't want to have to deal with that. We may want the new behavior, but we want it for free.

When I'm helping clients find solutions for their problems I often say, "Let's look at your options."

One client I had was sharing her home with her aunt. The client (I'll call her "Rose") was a single mom with three children, and her aunt ("Violet") took care of them during the day while her niece worked. It had seemed like a good solution for all concerned when they started the arrangement.

They came to me when things turned sour. Rose, a nutritionist, was angry at the foods Violet gave her children, particularly junk foods. Violet insisted, "All kids eat hamburgers and fries at fast food places. And a stop at the Dairy Queen every day lets them know they're loved."

There were multiple other differences in their parenting styles, and both women were firm in their beliefs. I could see that each one wanted me to take her side and simply say, "Rose is right" or "Violet's right."

Of course I couldn't, because, though I have my own beliefs, they're not chiseled in stone as correct truths.

All I could do was help both women define their options and then make the decisions which seemed best for them.

"Rose and Violet, are there any advantages to this current living arrangement?"

"Oh, sure," they agreed quickly. Rose knew Violet loved her kids fiercely and took excellent care of them in the long run, and Violet could stretch her retirement income by having no rent to pay.

"Good," I agreed. "And did you agree on certain ground rules in the beginning?"

The answer was no, of course, because both had assumed the other "knew" the right way to raise children.

"Okay, so it took a while for the problems to surface, but now that they have can you agree on some ground rules?"

Both women frowned and dug their heels in. It was clear each wanted the other to change her beliefs.

"Well, then," I said, "It seems pretty clear that you're both going to be unhappy unless you can come to some agreement. If you can do that, things will smooth out. If you can't you may have to end the living arrangement. Which way do you both think you want to go?"

Only if both say they're willing to find a workable compromise can we begin negotiating.

Lee: Rose, what's one of the things you'd like Violet to change in the way she cares for your kids?

Rose: No more junk food!

Lee: Violet, are you willing to agree to that?

Violet: No way. It's too restrictive. I did a good job raising my own kids. They're grown up and healthy. I don't want to be bossed around about what I feed kids.

Lee: Are you willing to make any changes?

Violet: Well, maybe I could limit our trips to McDonald's and the Dairy Queen. Say, to three times a week.

Rose: Once a week I could tolerate.

Violet: Too restrictive.

Lee: How about twice a week?

Reluctantly both agree to that. And so we continue. Except it rarely goes that smoothly. It might take 30 or 40 minutes to arrive at that one compromise, with both parties explaining over and over why they believe they're right. It could even take three or four sessions, or twelve or twenty.

I try to stop the repeating of arguments. They've already said a million times why they believe a certain way, and it clearly hasn't changed the other's mind, so it's wasting time to repeat them any further.

But all of us have to come to the bottom line of a problem: What are my choices, and what do I want to do about them? Remember we can't make the other person change, only ourselves.

So whether my problem involves only myself (as in the continuous song in my mind) or another person as well, it always comes down to my options. Often we're so close to our difficulties we can't see the whole picture clearly, and it may take some time before we can come to terms with the simple, bare-boned possibilities.

Should I put my efforts in on getting rid of the tune or accept it and enjoy the music? Should I send away my aunt and find a different sitter or accept her and her ways? Of course we may be able to negotiate and compromise, but the question is still, "Can this be changed or do I need to accept it?"

Sometimes acceptance can be beautifully comfortable if that's the route we choose. Coming to terms with "I can't change this person, but I can love what's good about him and accept the not-so-good" is freeing. It takes away the frustration of constantly wishing he would change, which can be very burdensome, indeed.

If you, like I, have ever wanted someone to change so much that you find yourself constantly watching him for "improvement," you're just as constantly setting yourself up for more disappointment when nothing happens.

It's kind of like wanting to run a marathon. I'm not a runner, but if I decided to become one I might set my sights on a marathon a year or two from now and begin to train. I'd walk. Every day. I'd walk, I'd stretch, I'd exercise, I'd pant, I'd rest, I'd run. I'd shower and run some more. I might get a trainer. I might find a friend to run with. I'd eat properly, take my pulse, keep increasing my running time and distance. I'd work like a dog.

Many times in that effort I'd feel discouraged. I'd no doubt consider giving up the idea, but I'd convince myself of its worth, and try harder. Perhaps the progress I'd make would feed my enthusiasm, and I'd come to enjoy the process thoroughly. That'd be great.

But if I found myself questioning more and more why I ever decided to attempt a marathon, if discouragement became a frequent companion, and I were more and more dispirited and disheartened, I might decide to accept a different goal for myself. Perhaps a half marathon would suffice, or maybe a 10K.

It's my decision, no one else's. Looking at the choices open to me, being at a crossroads, I'd weigh how I'd probably feel with each.

Would my pride at continuing and reaching my first goal make it all worthwhile? Or would the joy I'd feel at changing my goal bring me peace of mind and contentment?

I already know the answer I'd come to, being such a creature of comfort. Accepting the lesser goal would make me ecstatic. I would experience the utmost bliss at reveling in the knowledge that I'd let myself off the agony hook!

But you might feel unbounded joy at your decision to continuing striving and experiencing the exhilaration of reaching a long-awaited and hard-won victory.

Again the question to decide is "Do I keep working to change the status quo or accept something else?"

Years and years ago Alcoholics Anonymous adopted the Prayer of St. Francis for its members: God, grant me the serenity to accept the things I cannot change, courage to change the things I can, and wisdom to know the difference.

But, oh, that's the hard part, that "wisdom to know the difference." Most of us have serenity and/or courage at our beck and call, but that wisdom is on shaky ground. How can we be sure of the wisest choice?

Again, we can't. So many questions in life have no clear cut, black or white answer. Probably either choice would work. One way might have a better set of results, but it may also have some uncomfortable consequences we can't foresee at the moment.

We usually underestimate our strength in dealing with whatever challenges we face, and we overestimate their seriousness. I love the old saying, "It's almost impossible to overestimate the unimportance of practically anything."

Sometimes I subscribe to the advice that goes, "If you're not sure, do nothing."

Other times I prefer the adage, "When you're faced with two choices, one of which is a risk of some sort, take the risky one. It'll make you grow." Sooner or later we usually pick one, and we feel relieved.

But often we're still not over the hump. We may continue vacillating, wondering if we made a mistake and should reverse that decision. Generally we can, and if we do we might find ourselves regretting that one. Sometimes we may chase our tails around and around, driving ourselves nearly crazy with doubts.

The reason is that we want the choice to bring us happiness, and few things in life are without disappointments. So when some shadow appears we immediately think we must have chosen the wrong option, when, in fact, the other one might have been just as trying for us.

In the end we choose our poison. I can live with some circumstances that someone else would find too appalling to consider, and vice versa. So all I can do is do my best to make considered judgments and then try them on to see if they fit.

Society may frown on certain decisions because through the years it's been customary and expected to act in a certain way. Though it might take a lot of courage for us to go against society's approval, we like ourselves best when we do what we believe is right.

Okay, that's all well and good. But what if I make a choice, I choose my option, I feel good about the decision, I begin living with the change, and I find myself drifting back to the old way?

We all do that! Actually living with the "new me" is a lot harder than we'd thought it would be. We have to accept those setbacks which AA calls slips: resorting back to our old behavior when we've thought we were doing pretty well at the new. Suddenly we're back at square one.

That's how it feels, but we're really not starting from scratch again. We've made some headway, we've put a lot of energy into our change, and we're proud of the progress we've made. But changing an old habit is one of the most difficult challenges we undertake, so we must be prepared to accept setbacks.

I've known many alcoholics who go conscientiously to their weekly or even daily AA meetings, and finally they win their buttons for being abstinent for a whole year. They hear the applause from their fellow members, and they feel justifiably proud and strong as they return to their seats.

One client had celebrated her "first birthday" of abstinence and was continuing her AA attendance when she had a slip.

"It was a good morning," she told me. "I'd slept well, had a good breakfast, gone to work and finished doing it by noon. The boss told me to take the rest of the day off.

"I was delighted. I went to a crafts store for some new brushes and put them in my car. Instead of getting into the driver's seat I walked right back to the shopping center, went into a liquor store and bought a gallon of Chardonnay.

"Then I went home and drank it all. I went back to the liquor store for more, which I drank, and I stayed drunk for four days. Finally I couldn't even get out of bed. I just laid there, peeing in the bed, drinking, passing out, waking up to drink some more. Finally one of my friends came to check on me."

As she told me about her episode she looked like death. Her skin was almost grey, her face puffy and her eyes full of shame and despair. I felt so sorry for her. But still I had not a shred of doubt that this was just a slip, and I knew she could get back on the wagon and back in shape. Which she did. In a few days she was once again the bright, happy, lovely travel agent I'd come to know.

She still goes to AA and stays in close touch with her sponsor. She plans not to slip again, but she might. And if she does she can get herself off alcohol and back in shape. It happens. It's not a horrible sin, and we needn't beat ourselves up for it, whether our journey is with alcohol or anything else.

A delightful couple I know struggled with anger and disrespect. We worked together, off and on, for some time, and I'd explain how damaging their treatment of each other was. We did role playing, with me yelling insults at them as a demonstration of what not to do. We did exercises in respectful communication. We practiced my favorite little formula for conflict resolution: When you ____, I feel ____ because____. Would you be willing to ____?

We watched body language and practiced active listening. They'd leave each session with new resolve to continue conversing the ways we'd agreed upon, but in a matter of weeks (or days, sometimes) they'd fall back into their disrespect at each other. Either one might start it, but in no time the other had joined in. The yelling would escalate until it would seem like there was utter hatred between them instead of the love I knew they felt for one another.

I haven't seen them for some time, and I always hope that's a good sign; that they're doing well at their challenge. But I know they have at least these three strong options open to them:

One, they can maintain the status quo and continue living their married life in anger and unhappiness.

Two, they can split. They can get a divorce and look for someone else to marry, with whom they're likely to continue their terribly disrespectful patterns of communication.

Three, they can determine they're going to change their bad habit and begin communicating respectfully. I do know this: they can do it! It's definitely harder for some people than for others, but each one of us can learn and practice good communication skills. If we want to.

There are folks, however, who don't really want to change; they want only their mates to change. Unless they make the choice to really apply themselves, they won't be conscientious in working at it. So those people will live their lives as yellers and screamers. Some of those marriages continue to work, though, when both are so used to that lifestyle they've developed a high tolerance for insults.

Some of them admit to a certain pleasure they take in "letting off steam" and then making up. It works for them.

I guess it's like the "song in their heads" that they've lived with so long they've come to feel almost comfortable with it. Once they decide they'd rather live with it than try to change it they can live happily ever after, too…enjoying the music, so to speak.

It wouldn't be the choice I'd make, that's for sure, but each of us has our boundaries, and that's okay. But what if one of you is willing and dedicated to changing your behavior and the other isn't? That's certainly not fair, is it?

Sadly that's not a rare situation; it's far more common than both parties being in agreement. And that just brings up another option opportunity. (An op op, if you will.)

Let's go back to Rose and Violet with this one.

Violet is willing to curb her overly nurturing habits but not to stop them entirely. Rose says that's unacceptable. Violet says okay, then, she's getting her own place and Rose is on her own.

Next day at breakfast Rose watches Violet pack her things and begins to recognize the difficulty she's going to face in finding sitters. By the time the kids are brushing their teeth Rose speaks, tentatively.

"Violet?"

"What?"

"I don't know what I'm going to do."

"I don't know what you're going to do, either," says Violet, crisply, and continues packing.

"Who's going to pick up the kids?"

"Beats me, Rose."

Silence follows as Rose sips her coffee.

Then she speaks again.

"Violet?"

"Hm?"

"I guess I'm willing to let you feed the kids the way you want to, if you'd be willing to stay. I know I've made a big fuss over it, but in the long run I believe they're way better off with you than with some stranger."

Enjoying her position, Violet might silently continue to pack for a few minutes before she says, "If you mean that, then I'll stay."

Rose is vastly relieved. The price of being solely responsible for her children is too expensive for her mental health. She knows they love Auntie Violet and she loves them, and that's what matters most.

She was able to see her options differently enough to change her mind.

All of us would benefit by checking out our own options when we're dealing with a problem. We're so used to reacting in the same, predictable ways that we can easily overlook all the other choices open to us.

We seem to have tunnel vision in searching for solutions. A client of mine wishes her husband would spend more time with the family than he does. (In fact, probably most of my female clients wish their husbands would spend more time with their families!)

Each time she comes for a session she begins the recitation of all the ways her mate "wasted time" that could have been spent with the children and her. Her belief seems to be something like, "If I give Lee enough information about his transgressions she'll be able to get him to change."

I understand her thinking. Goodness knows I've spent enough time trying to get my husband to change his ways! That's how I know it doesn't work. Nobody is going to change behavior because someone wants them to.

She says, "But if he loved me, wouldn't he want to become the way I want him to be?"

I explain that he could say the same thing. "If she loved me, she'd want to become what I want her to be."

Then it takes on a more global spin; a moral and ethical view. "But men are supposed to spend time with their families. All the articles say that. That's what's wrong with the world today, our pastor says. People don't have enough family time together."

Be that as it may, apparently her husband isn't concerned about it; at least not enough to make that happen, so I point that out. That simply adds to her frustration, and she says impatiently, "Well, but he should!"

Quite honestly I think he should, too. And I've talked to him about that very thing when he's been here, but he thinks he spends more than enough time with the family. So if she's told him and I've told him and the pastor's told him and "all the magazines" have told him, then why isn't he doing it?

Because he doesn't want to. Either he's able to convince himself that his family doesn't need him around, or he's deliberately refusing to cooperate just to prove to her she can't control him or there's some other reason altogether. Who knows? He says he spends enough time with them and he won't change and that's that.

Okay, so it's an option opportunity, an op op. All she and I can do at our sessions is look at her options and let her decide which she wants. Or at least which one is the least uncomfortable for her.

Probably none will feel comfortable.

Let's think of some of her alternatives, and we'll let our imaginations run wild just for fun. Let's see, she could divorce him. She could hire a man to play the father's role around the home. She could accept the concept that the kids will grow up without a father's presence. She might tell the kids he's a jerk with bad values. She might tell all her friends and neighbors the same thing. She could ask the pastor to talk to him. (Actually she did, and he did, and nothing changed.) She could spend the rest of their married life nagging him and trying to get him to see the light. She could find still another counselor who might be able to change him. And so on.

She and I have talked about this for some time now, and her choice is always the same: get him to change.

I've been honest with her and said, "Since that's the option you consistently choose, and it's something I can't do for you, you're wasting money if you keep coming to me for help with this. Of course I'm willing to keep seeing you if you get anything out of these sessions, but it seems to me you're not benefitting much from them. No one that I know will ever be able to change the man."

"I like to come here. At least I get to vent and I always feel understood, and I feel better when I leave," she responds.

And so she continues to come. Sometimes I feel a little uncomfortable, like I'm taking her money under false pretenses. But they're not false, since I've been totally honest with her. I'm taking her money because she likes to come.

She compares our sessions to her manicures and massages. "Those can't help me deal with him, either," she says, "but they make me feel better. At least I get to complain about him for an hour."

When it's time for my own op op I come up with these options: I can terminate our counseling relationship, perhaps referring her to another counselor. I can tell her she's wasting my time and I don't like seeing her anymore. I can lie and say, "Maybe he is going to change after all." I can wish she would "get it" and change her expectations.

Or I can accept her on her terms. I can acknowledge the fact that she prefers maintaining the status quo within her family, and I can sit back and listen to her stories.

Once I change my expectations (that I help her find solutions) I feel no more stress about the prospect of trying to help her. Changing my expectations about anything changes the way I feel. I become un-stuck. I'm free from stress.

It sounds so easy: "Just change your expectations." In fact it's one of the most difficult tasks we take on, but it's so worth it when it finally clicks. Like everything else we've learned, practice makes the process easier. So the more I work on changing expectations, the more easily I find myself doing it.

Of course there are a lot of expectations we don't have to change because what we expect always happens. Those we take for granted. I expect my family to give me hugs when I see them, and, sure enough, they always do. I expect a good haircut when I sit down in Minerva's chair, and I always get one. We sure don't need or want to change those expectations.

But the ones that do need altering are the ones which keep disappointing us. We might wonder why in the world we keep hoping and expecting some behavior from someone who's already shown us many times that we're not going to get different behavior, but I guess it's hard to give up old wishes and dreams.

Mama used to say, "Hurt me once, shame on you. Hurt me twice, shame on me." In other words, I should know what to expect after you've hurt me the first time. I should but I don't. At least not for a while. Not until I get so sick and tired of hoping and being disappointed that I finally hit my forehead and say, "I get it!" Ah, an op op. Now I'll get around to checking what options are available to me, and then I'm halfway there. Now I can change my direction, fine tune my hopes, welcome back my self-reliance, and settle back to enjoy my music.

ten

God

Every movie has an executive producer. He's the source that makes it happen. Perhaps his primary task is finding the funds without which it wouldn't happen at all, but in addition he brings all the necessary people together: the writers, director, editor and actors.

Throughout the creation of the film it's his job to oversee the relationships among all those folks and give them some direction. Without his guidance there would no doubt be chaos, as each individual would try to have everything go his own way. The executive producer lends continuity and cohesiveness to the entire process and the whole crew recognizes his power.

So it is in our personal movies. I get to be the star of my production as well as the writer, editor, director and shooter, but my movie wouldn't be made at all if there weren't an executive producer behind me. My relationship with him is vitally important because of his ultimate power.

He's laid down some rules for the success of this movie, but he's also given me a tremendous amount of creative license. He doesn't nag me or "pull rank" and insist I do things his way, but he's provided a whole heap of memos in this world to help me concoct the most rewarding movie possible. Whether I take his advice is up to me, and I certainly can't blame him for my failures if I've ignored it.

Lewis B. Mayer, Samuel Goldwyn, David O. Selznick, Steven Spielberg, and a host of others have left their legacies on screen. In developing our own movies, however, we've got the best executive producer around: God.

As I write this I'm aware of a bit of uncertainty as to whether I should tackle the subject of God, and yet I can't write a book about happiness and joy without including him. If, however, you feel offended at my presumptions, don't hesitate to skip this chapter. Remember, you're in control of your movie—and that includes reading what you want and ignoring the rest.

I'm aware that the very word "God" is a turn-off to some people. In fact I had a chuckle recently when a local church called me to speak on self-esteem at one of their group meetings. The person who called said, "We're an unusual Protestant church, you know. We're made up of Catholics, Jews and 'Others,' which includes many agnostics. Some people bristle at the 'G-word,' but feel free to talk about spirituality, because everyone here is comfortable with that term."

It seemed unusual, to say the least, that a church group had to be wary of "the G word," but the gentleman gave me permission to use it. He encouraged me to say whatever I felt comfortable talking about, but to be forewarned in case there were objections.

The various twelve-step programs have made the term "higher power" popular, and it's a good, descriptive expression. Yet I run across some people who find even that unpalatable, and they have a stumbling block in working through the twelve steps. Some of them think of "Nature." A few use "The combined power of this group." But Alcoholics Anonymous and all the other related programs began with "God as you know Him," and now may substitute "Higher Power."

Whatever works for you is fine with me, but I'm concerned if you don't believe in anything outside yourself, because life's mighty tough that way.

I've had only one client who committed suicide, and my heart went out to her for months before that happened. She not only didn't believe in God or any higher power, she also had all the money she could ever want. That's when I realized what powerful motivators God and money are.

Most of us need money and we work, "marry well" or find another way to get that need met. At least it provides some motivation for us as we go about the business of living.

There are a few for whom money is not an issue at all, but generally most people have some moral and ethical values that help shape their lives. A person who has no needs to meet and who can find no reason for living is in a tragic and vulnerable position indeed, and for my client suicide seemed the best solution to her emptiness.

I have several really close friends, however, who don't believe in God, and they seem perfectly content with their lives. I never argue with success. If you're happy, you're probably doing what's best for you. If you're not, you might want to consider other options.

One option is prayer. I personally agree with Thoreau, who said, "More things are wrought by prayer than this world dreams of."

What is prayer? Just simply communicating. Communication is the only tool we have in relating to each other here on earth, and it's also how we relate to God. (The church people I mentioned who avoid "the G word" also prefer not to use "the P word." They substitute "energy" for "prayer." Whatever works.)

Sometimes I ask clients, "Do you believe in God?" And often they look a little uncomfortable and say, "Well, I don't go to church."

I think those are two very separate issues, myself. One can believe in God and never set foot inside a church or synagogue or mosque.

Many people say, "I believe in something, but I can't imagine that it's involved or concerned with me as a person. It's like a force of nature that has created the world, but not someone who sits up there and watches me."

I rarely try to change anyone's mind, but I'm grateful that I believe God does "sit up there and watch me." I think, in fact, he loves me terribly much and thinks I'm wonderful! And he feels the same about you.

So to me praying is simple, because it's easy to talk to someone who loves you and thinks you're wonderful, isn't it? We all love people who accept us unconditionally and continue to love us in spite of our mistakes.

For me, prayer is just talking to God like I would to you if you were here in this room with me. I wouldn't be formal at all with you, and I'm not with him either. No thees or thous in my chats with God. I just say things I would say to a loving parent, and in the same way. I might think, "Wow, God, thanks for letting me be here on vacation with my whole family. It is so much fun being together, and thanks for that sunset over the ocean, too. Help me not make a pig of myself at dinner tonight. Help me use a little restraint and not order dessert even if everyone else does."

If God created me there's no doubt that he understands my thinking, so I don't have to worry that my prayers are flawed or less than perfect. Of course they're way less than perfect, but who cares? Certainly not God. I think he's just tickled to death when we talk to him at all, and he's not grading us like a stern schoolteacher circling our errors in red. Rather he hears what we're feeling and thinking even though our words may be simple.

The process of communicating with God has gotten way more complicated than it needs to be, in my opinion. The mechanics of prayer don't matter nearly as much as just simply doing it. I've seen dozens of books in stores advising "How to Pray," or something similar, implying there are rules or guidelines or standards we must know and follow to get the job done. We don't need how-to's teaching us to converse with people who love us. If they love us they're open to whatever we have to say, and in God's case we don't even have to verbalize it; we may simply think it.

The kind of love that's most like God's, I'm guessing, is a parent's love, only God's is way better. He has so much confidence in our abilities that he doesn't have to stew about our behavior like our parents did. I've no doubt he feels concern for us while we're in the midst of messing up, but I'll bet he doesn't despair like mortal parents can. He often lets us stew in our own juices for long periods of time, knowing we're learning something from the process. And he has his arms around us the whole time.

Some people wonder whether God could ever forgive them for something they've done in the past. With clients who feel that way, I love to share a hand-me-down story that was first written by one of the great theologians.

It is said that we're all issued new white robes the minute we're born. Some of us put ours on immediately and begin to live life. As we proceed through months and years of living our robes begin to show some wear and tear. We take risks and make mistakes in judgment. The robes get dirty and ripped from time to time. The more adventurously we live, the more beat-up our robes become. From time to time we wash them out, mend them the best we can, and put them on them again.

Other people save their new white robes, leaving them inside the cellophane bags in which they were issued. They wear sensible clothes and make sensible decisions. All their behavior is carefully thought out, and they almost never take risks of any kind. Therefore their mistakes are minimal and usually caused by those other people in the dirty robes who are being careless. Now and then the "good" people open their cedar chests and carefully remove the neatly packaged robes, wondering when there will be an occasion important enough to warrant wearing them.

It turns out that when we pass from this world to the next we're supposed to show up in our white robes. Imagine the delight of the "good" people, who now get dressed in their pristine garments and proceed cautiously (for they are always cautious) up to the pearly gates. How proud they feel as they see the others, hurrying up in robes they should be ashamed of. Their robes are so soiled and stained that no amount of washing could ever make them white again, and look how they hang in tatters!

Then God appears. With the greatest of love in his manner, he opens up the gate and invites everybody in. And in the gentlest of tones he praises the folks wearing the dirty, raggedy robes, saying, "You people really lived life! You tasted everything I put into the world. You took risks, you made millions of mistakes, most of which you learned from. I know a lot of your decisions brought you pain, but you lived your entire life with courage and enthusiasm. Good for you!"

I would hope I'm one of the ones with the disgraceful-looking robes when I get to those gates. Life offers so many wonderful experiences that surely the biggest mistake of all would be living so cautiously we miss most of the adventure.

I tell this story when a client or a friend is feeling a lot of guilt and can't seem to shake it. They've made some error in judgment, done something they really regret, and they're steeped in the misery of having erred so seriously.

Often I ask if they believe in God, and if they do I ask if they think God would forgive them. Usually they believe God has forgiven them, but they still can't forgive themselves. That's when I tell them about the white robes, and it gives them a different perspective on mistakes and risk-taking as well as God's continuing love for us. It often brings them a great deal of relief.

I've learned I need to be careful with that story, though, because it can be interpreted as permission to do whatever one wants.

I had a young woman client who was having an affair with her boss, a married man. He was one of those outrageously charming but devious fellows to whom women are often attracted even though we know what jerks they are. Most women have known at least one: a self-centered, dishonest, totally undependable guy, but he's so endearing and lighthearted that life is one big circus when he's around.

My client, Krista, was wasting precious years by seeing this man when she could have been "in the market" for a potential husband, and she was uncomfortably aware of that. Moreover she felt extremely guilty for cheating with him, because she knew and liked his wife as well. All things considered, she had decided to end their affair.

Having been raised Baptist, she had a strong moral belief system, and she was crying in my office as she bemoaned her recent sinful behavior.

"I've done everything wrong lately, and I'm so ashamed," she said. "I knew better than to get involved with him. It started out as just a flirtation, and I don't know how it got out of hand. I hate myself for betraying the trust I know his wife has in me."

Grateful for a tool with which to help her, I told her about the white robes, and sure enough she listened intently and started to smile. By the time she left she was feeling much better and was going back to the office to tell her boss she was leaving and why.

She called me a few days later and said, "Lee, I want to thank you so much for what you did last week. I thought about the white robe story on my way back to the office and realized it's okay for me to take risks and make mistakes, because God will love me anyway. So I'm going to continue the affair for a while because it's so much fun!"

Whoa.

I felt a rock in the pit of my stomach. "What did I do?" I thought. "Have I given Krista the impression she can do anything and it's all right? Furthermore now she thinks she has permission from her therapist!"

Suddenly I was right back in third grade hearing Sister Mary Domitilla saying, "If you give someone else permission to sin, God will surely hold you accountable for their sins."

"Wait a minute here, God," I thought. "I didn't know she was going to take it that way." Fortunately we had another appointment scheduled in a few days and I was able to share my thoughts with Krista again. I can't tell you how relieved I was when she ended the affair a week or so later, and I've been less inclined to tell the story since.

So why am I telling it here? Because I still believe it…but there are a few catches to it. I believe that all things work for good for those who love God, and that he will continue to forgive us and love us in spite of our errors in living. But, those mistakes still have their own natural and logical consequences. Almost every single thing I do has some effect on someone else, and we're not allowed to hurt each other.

We're not supposed to hurt anyone, including ourselves. Krista was hurting not only the boss's wife but the boss as well by encouraging him to cheat. Obviously she was harming herself. All those wrongs will mar the quality of her life on a logical basis, even if we leave God's teachings out of this. Any way you look at it, the combined behavior of Krista and her boss is doing damage to at least three people (and more if he has children). Perhaps even the other people in the office were being adversely affected.

Another aspect of our behavior is the impression it gives the others in our life, sometimes being a kind of contagious permission. The more we see our friends and co-workers having affairs the more we can begin to think, "Oh, what the heck, everybody else does it, why not me?" It's almost scary how fragile we are, how open to suggestion—especially when it appeals to the desire for fun and excitement and attention.

But there, again, God can help us. And too often, we get so wrapped up in everyday worries that we lose sight of how much he cares.

We used to have a little dog named Noel, who arrived at Christmas, and she loved visiting my parents in Winslow. She loved *being* there, but she hated *going* there. When we'd get out our suitcases and start to pack, Noel would lie down nearby and radiate anxiety. Her body language was full of fear and helplessness, because she knew it was all leading up to her being put into the car with us. Now a lot of dogs just love to ride, but Noel seemed to believe it was a fate worse than death. The minute the car doors closed she'd begin to whine and cling to any passenger who might rescue her.

We'd soothe and reassure her, trying to quiet her whimpering, and eventually after we'd driven for a half hour or so she'd lie down and go to sleep. But the second the car stopped she was startled awake and fearful again, and it would take another long period of motion to lull her to sleep. Since it's a six-hour between Tucson and Winslow, we all dreaded the trip.

"If only she could realize the big treat that's in store for her," we'd say, knowing my parents treated her like a princess. Of course once we got there she was all tail-wagging and jumping with joy, but she never relaxed and enjoyed the trip in the fourteen years we had her.

Often it occurred to us that God may feel about us as we felt about Noel. He probably thinks, "If only they'd just relax and enjoy this trip they'd be a lot happier!" But we're so busy whining and worrying, we keep ourselves miserable.

Then we look back and reflect how well things turned out "after all."

"I wish I hadn't wasted all that time worrying that I'd never get a job as a TV reporter," said Lisa after she'd been one for a few years. "I should have known God was steering me in some good direction."

Not that God always steers us toward the goal we have in mind, but it's amazing how things work out for us, often much better than the way we'd had it pictured. We do have tremendous freedom in our life decisions, however, and he can still make everything work out well in the long run.

When our children were small one of their favorite Disneyland attractions was the boat rides, a place in which they got to "drive" little boats around a good-size area. They look back now and smile at their naïveté in those days, believing then they were actually responsible for where the boats went. At some point they'd discover the boats were following tracks, and all their intense steering was just for fun.

Now they see their lives somewhat like that, enjoying having some leeway in their day to day decisions, but knowing God is keeping them neatly on the track if they'll only let him.

Not that I believe in pre-destination, in which everything is planned for us and we really have no say in anything. But I do think God is always taking care of us even when we're going in the wrong direction—if we want him to.

I also believe he gives us the freedom to make that important decision, knowing some of us are going to say, "Hey, who needs him? I can run my life very well without him, thank you." As a parent I can imagine how devastated I'd be if one of my kids chose to disregard me, and yet God continues to love people even after they've rejected him.

He knows, of course, why they've made that decision, and from his vantage point he understands. And

I'm convinced that he welcomes them back with open arms if they ever decide to go in that direction.

Some have been hurt so badly by an incident in their past that they can't conceive of a God allowing that to happen. They shut off any connection to him as a kind of defense, afraid to trust lest something like that happen to them again.

Others have seen hypocrisy in so-called "religious" people and so turn away from the whole system in disgust.

But many still have a small voice within them that wonders, "Could I be wrong? Might there really be a God?" And at some time in their lives they may find themselves willing to try finding out. For those I offer one of my favorite quotes: Those who seek God have already found him.

I've experienced God's help many times. A few years ago I went to the doctor complaining about how tired I'd been feeling, and it didn't take him long to discover colon cancer. When I heard the diagnosis I felt a tremendous jolt of disbelief, followed instantly by this realization: Well, I've always thought finding out you have cancer must be one of the worst things that can happen to you. I've just found it out, so now I know I can survive that step, anyhow.

Throughout the surgery I continued feeling pretty positive, although physically uncomfortable, but not very bad emotionally. When I found out it had spread to some lymph nodes I felt a wave of fear and discouragement, but I somehow also knew God was taking good care of me.

The worst times were during the chemotherapy when I would feel fatigued and nauseous, and sometimes during one of those bouts I'd hit bottom. I'd feel a real sense of despair, discouragement and anxiety, and the only thing I knew to do was ask God for help. "Please, dear God," I'd say fervently, "Please make me feel better and give me some peace of mind. If I could just relax and trust that you're taking care of me I know I'd feel better."

And I would inevitably feel relief. By the end of my year of chemotherapy I was so much closer to God than I had been, that I can look back and truly feel that getting cancer was one of the many good things that have happened to me. I'd always believed in God and had prayed with some regularity my whole life, but it was through that ordeal I became really close to him. I began to feel his love for me, not just accept the fact that he loves everybody.

eleven

What Gets in the Way?

I'm lucky to have a husband who freely gives me permission to quote him in my books. When I asked Larry, "What gets in the way of your being happy?" he thought for only a minute before answering, "Me."

"I don't let myself be happy much of the time," he explained. "That's why I enjoy being around our grandkids. I have permission to be childlike when I'm with them and when I'm in Disneyland."

He's taken a lot of kidding over the years about his inordinate love for Disneyland, a place he's visited over a hundred times. But he says, "It's a place where I feel completely free, without any cares at all. There's no other place in the world where I can feel that." When he puts it that way I understand, and if it made me feel that way I'd want to go all the time, too.

"The rest of the time I have to be serious," he went on, "or I feel like I have to be. It's just the way I see myself. I'm worthwhile only if I'm working hard or worried or anxiously trying to be responsible. I have to be controlled. I don't let myself be free and lighthearted unless I'm on vacation or in a situation in which I give myself permission to let go of responsibility."

I appreciate his candor and his willingness to explore his mind. And I admire his easy admission of what he sees as an old "parent tape." We all have them, and they continue to direct our lives long after they were delivered to us. As most of us do with our first child, Larry's parents began instilling in him the values of doing his best, working hard, striving for perfection, and always being responsible. As though it were recorded on tape the message has stayed in his mind for eighty-four years, and he feels guilty if he has too much fun. More than he would like to, he subscribes to an almost unconscious belief that "Life is a serious business."

What are the old tapes that the rest of us play constantly in our heads? Many share the same one Larry's describing, but we all have our variations. And by the time we're aware of them we're so used to living our lives built around them, it's unthinkable to replace them with other messages.

Could Larry, at this point in his life, change the tape to "Life is a place where it's good to have fun and feel lighthearted?" Without a doubt. But he might not want to make the effort.

It would depend on how much he's enjoying his life the way it is, and he seems to be liking it just fine. It works for him. It might not for you or me, but that isn't the issue. That's the great part about being in charge of our own movies; we get to figure out what feels best to us and go after it.

If I were the director in Larry's movie I'd make dozens of changes. I'd like being the writer, as well, so I could completely rewrite his script. (Well, not completely—I'd still have him marry me.) I'd take over his entire life if he'd but say the word, and I'd love every second of it.

Fortunately for both of us he's not about to say the word, so I don't have to/get to "play God."

I do, however, have complete say in my own movie, and that's a big enough challenge in itself.

And so do you. You get to answer the question I posed to Larry for yourself. What gets in the way of your being happy?

Sometimes it's not an easy answer to come up with. I remember a comment my father made years ago when he was very unhappy with his life. We called him "Weed," a nickname he'd enjoyed for many years. He used to say proudly that weeds could survive in spite of great adversity, and that you just couldn't get rid of them no matter how you tried. But he'd lost my mother a few years before and turned to alcohol for solace. When drinking became a problem he went through a treatment center and quit, but he had nothing to take its place.

Cataracts and glaucoma complicated his sight, and cigarettes affected his circulation so badly that finally both his legs had to be amputated. This little scrap of a man would sit in his wheelchair or on his bed in the nursing home and wait for someone to sit with him so he could smoke, which was the only pleasure he had left.

Larry and I would visit him daily and try to think of things that might brighten his day. I was always saying something like, "I'll take this old picture album; that will tickle him." But he never felt tickled. Larry would read aloud to him or turn on the World Series for them to watch together, and my father would thank him graciously, but he never seemed to enjoy the games. Nor the books, the pictures, or the conversations. Only the cigarettes seemed to bring him comfort, but not pleasure. It was one of the hardest times I've had to face.

Several times he had diseases that were life-threatening, but he always pulled through. During one of those I was holding his hand, watching his eyes with their vacant, preoccupied expression, and wishing I could see the spark that used to be there. It seemed like he didn't really want to be alive anymore. One day I found the courage to ask him gently, "Do you sometimes wish you could just be free of all this, Weed? Would you rather be in Heaven with Mama?"

He thought for a minute while I held my breath, and then he answered: "I don't want to die. But I don't want to live. I just want everything to go smooth."

I couldn't help smiling at him, understanding that he didn't know what would make him happy anymore. And it wasn't too much longer before he did let go of that pretty miserable existence and join all the people he'd loved here who'd preceded him to Heaven.

All of us cried and missed him, but we were relieved for him.

I've thought of his statement many times, though, when I see people who seem stuck in an unhappy place but don't feel like making the effort necessary to make change happen. They, too, "don't want to live and don't want to die; they just want everything to go smooth."

And life so rarely runs smoothly!

Fortunately we don't usually see our situations as matters of life and death, but let's use that idea and change the words to "accept or change." Too often we don't want to do either. We just want things to be smooth, to be easier. In essence it usually boils down to "I just want other people to change their behavior."

Therein lies the rub. I am the star of my movie, and the writer, director and producer, but I often forget that all the other people are enjoying writing and starring in their own movies. They're not going to play a role in mine the way I might write it for them.

They might consent to being actors in it, but they won't be willing to become the characters I've envisioned them to be.

My happiness in dealing with them, then, is determined by my willingness to let them be who they are. The more I refuse to accept them that way, the unhappier I make myself.

One might think I'd have figured that out long ago and would have stopped expecting them to "be different" by now. Would that were true! I'd be happy as a lark.

It's only when I want someone to act differently, and I begin to depend on their doing that, that I get upset. It's my dependency that gets in my way, not their behavior.

How can I tell how dependent I am? It's so simple. It's how unhappy I am. That's a good thermometer for me to consult anytime I'm discouraged or depressed or disappointed. In fact every time I'm disappointed I've been depending on somebody for something. If I weren't dependent I'd have no negative feelings about that particular relationship.

I've found it a foolproof rule, and I'll bet you will, too. Just for fun, jot down some things you wish were different about your life. They might be things like "I wish I could find my old roommate, Carol Poole." "I wish Larry enjoyed working in the yard with me." "I wish my nieces and nephews would send me e-mail more often."

In every case I have no power; only the others involved have.

I tried to find Carol. I even hired a "finder" to find her. He was defeated because her last name is no longer the ones by which I knew her. I can wish Carol would try to find me. (I'm right here where I always was.) But I can do no more to make that happen than I've already done. I either have to accept that or change my behavior and stop wishing. I can't change Carol.

I wish Larry liked yard work. But we've discussed that some 10,000 times in our 60-year marriage, so when am I going to accept the fact that he didn't and he doesn't and he won't? If I ever do I'll be happy. I'll be free of wishes and expectations and dependency—that one, anyway.

As to my nephews and nieces and e-mail—well, they'll write as often as they feel like it. If frequent communications were important to me I could be upset when I don't get them. Fortunately that's not a dependency for me. I'm pleased when I hear from them and content when I don't.

That is how I'd like to feel about almost everything.

Suppose it's a situation about which I do care strongly, and I have negative feelings much of the time because of it. Realizing that I wouldn't be sad if it weren't a dependency I'd developed, I'm free to solve my problem (for it is mine) any way I want.

An example: I had a very close friend whom I valued deeply for several years. We seemed to have a lot in common, and we talked almost every day. Over the years we got to know each so well she seemed like the sister I never had. I loved her sense of humor, I enjoyed hearing the day-to-day happenings of her family and telling her about mine.

Eventually, however, I became aware she'd been backing off, distancing herself, being less interested in getting together. For a long time I explained it away by realizing she had a new job and new friendships developing there. But I missed her.

I wouldn't have thought of it as dependency, but clearly it was, or I wouldn't have felt the loss as deeply as I did. I finally talked to her about it, and she said she was aware of it and felt guilty for not calling.

I didn't want to pursue a friendship that was held up by "shoulds" on my friend's part. I wanted it to be mutually fun, or I'd rather not continue it.

So after a time I explained that to her, said I recognized the changes in her life and that I'd prefer we took a break for a while. The ball would be in her court, and if she wanted to get together she could call, but I'd no longer be trying to hold the friendship together.

We parted friends, and have been just "ordinary" friends ever since. If I run into her at the mall we're delighted to see each other, but I successfully got over my expectations that we'd always be such close friends. Then I felt okay about it.

"God grant me the serenity to accept the things I cannot change." Fortunately I had the wisdom to see that I couldn't change her priorities, only my expectations.

So what gets in the way of happiness? Wanting something I can't have and being unwilling to give up that desire. The harder I struggle to attain or achieve it the more pain I give myself.

Sometimes I feel real sympathy for clients whose spouses want out of their marriages for some reason. For many it's having found another person with whom to feel infatuated. The one who's "dumping" a spouse feels guilty, as a rule, but justifies it by saying, "My new lover and I never meant for it to happen. It just did. We just fell in love, and now we have to be together."

In the course of counseling I always ask the departing partner if he or she saw marriage as a permanent commitment, a sacred state. Their answers vary. Some say, "Oh, yes, I thought I'd stay in this marriage forever, but I just fell out of love."

Others say, "I knew I wasn't in love when I walked down the aisle at our wedding, but I figured it was too late to back out then."

One said, "I'm not happy with my mate anymore, and I can't believe God would want me to be unhappy!"

Whatever their rationales, it would be impossible for any counselor to "make" them stay with their current spouses, so I can only help the "dumpees" adjust to their loss and begin to carve out a new life.

I wish I had a nickel for every discarded spouse whom I see a few years later reporting happily, "You know, I never thought I'd be saying this, but I'm so much better off without ____. I learned I was quite capable of living independently, and now I like being so free. I get to make all my own decisions. I like being able to do what I want, when I want, mess up the house if I feel like it, just be *me*."

Sometimes they add, "And I'm seeing a new friend I met a few months ago. We have so much in common and such fun together!"

They're successful in ridding themselves of their previous dependencies.

By contrast some people stay stuck in a perpetual state of bitterness the rest of their lives. It's as though they're choosing to harbor their disappointment and rage, nurturing it by complaining to one and all how shabbily they were treated by their "Ex." They'd rather nurse their wounds, holding tightly to their dependencies, than release them and enjoy a new lifestyle.

It's their choice. It's our choice. It's our life, our movie, our chosen agenda. We have zero control over others, but lots and lots of control over ourselves.

twelve

Solutions

I've never heard of a movie where everything went smoothly from start to finish. Most of the movie-making stories I've heard describe misfortunes on the set, directors throwing up their hands in despair, actors bemoaning the day they ever agreed to perform, and all manner of problems before the movie ever makes it to the screen.

Solving problems takes a lot of trial-and-error experience. None of us is born with the skills we need in that department, so much of our childhood is spent trying various approaches, keeping some, discarding most.

I remember going to a dance recital in which our two daughters were performing when they were in grade school. In one of the numbers, two darling little girls (maybe six and eight years old) came onstage dressed in elaborate Spanish costumes. When the music began they did their dance steps with eager anticipation and the confidence that comes with lots of practice. All went well for a minute or two, but then the younger one faltered and lost her place. She looked to the older girl for rescuing, but couldn't figure out how to get back on track. She stood in frozen panic for what seemed like an eternity but which was probably thirty seconds, while the older girl continued to dance.

Suddenly that dancer realized it wasn't working and in a moment of heroic proportions did what she could to save the day. She grabbed her little partner's hand and began to run, around and around the stage. For the duration of the music they ran in a wild-eyed frenzy, faking their "dance" with brave, brilliant smiles, performing what seemed like the best solution they could come up with to assure that the show would go on.

Many times in my life I've done something equally laughable in a valiant effort to get through a difficult situation, trying as hard as they did to make it look like I was in complete control of the situation.

After the fact it's easy to look back and think of other behavior which would have been more sensible, but when we attempt any solution we at least deserve credit for trying.

I think many of us "run around the stage" in embarrassment when we're afraid and unsure of what's expected of us. We feel somehow we need to do something, and any activity is preferable to standing there looking like fools.

So we need to be kind to ourselves in our mistakes and not beat ourselves up for behavior that was well-intentioned but not too sound. It helps a lot to know that we can learn something valuable with each mistake we make, so no dumb behavior need be wasted. (Don't say "If only," say "next time.") Little by little we get better at coming up with good strategies, and there's a never-ending supply of fresh problems with which to practice.

If I'm the writer of my script for life I get to make the decisions about handling all my problems. Some people see that as a "have to" instead of a "get to," because it does put the responsibility squarely on self. It means I can no longer blame somebody else, darn it, and that was always so easy!

Sometimes I look back with nostalgia at the days when I blamed everyone else for my unhappiness. Usually it was Larry, because most of us tend to blame the person we're closest to when things aren't working well. (I admit, I still do!)

Actually many categories of people can fill the bill when we need to blame someone: bosses, co-workers, neighbors, our children, our parents, our friends…almost anybody. There are always politicians aplenty if we need to look further, and one of the nicest things about them as targets for our wrath is the ease with which we can find folks who'll agree with us.

Sometimes it's tremendously gratifying to play "Ain't it awful" with our friends, bad-mouthing the people in the news at the moment. We can recount with relish the stories in the paper and enjoy the warmth of "belonging" to the vast group of acquaintances who are equally shocked and disapproving of how "those people" behave.

All of that is normal and satisfying, and somehow it improves our state of mind because we can feel a smidgen superior, perhaps. We can say smugly, "Well, I could look as good as Elizabeth Taylor if I could afford as many face lifts as she's had."

Or "Hey, I knew enough not to vote for that guy for mayor, but he won anyway. Now the whole town can see I was right."

There's always, "In the old days kids weren't allowed to dress like that. The trouble with the country today is the attitude those kids have. Just look at that boy with the nose ring!"

Whatever. We have our favorite gripes, and we're probably not going to stop. But when we get tired of some specific problem we've been living with, we have to/get to look to ourselves for solutions.

It helps to define the problem as clearly as possible. Often we describe our problems so globally it's almost impossible to begin solving them.

We might say, "My marriage is bad." Or "I wish I had a job I liked." Or "I have bad self esteem, that's my problem." "I'm in rotten shape physically." "I have no self-discipline." "I let everybody take advantage of me." All very broad descriptions that seem larger than life, they're so vast they seem to defy solutions. Where would one begin?

The first step is coming to terms with the fact that I'm the one who needs to change. That may be the hardest part; we're so accustomed to believing it's the others who should do it. (Maybe they should, but they probably won't.)

Once I buy the concept that "if it is to be, it is up to me," I've passed the first hurdle. There's a good feeling that comes into play then, knowing that I've just taken over my life. I can now feel a sense of power that I was lacking before. Waiting and hoping for the other guy to change is a discouraging way of life, because it's usually futile. One feels helpless and that's because one is helpless as a subservient victim.

Conversely, when I determine I'm taking control of my life I no longer have to be the passive, whining, begging, sniveling wimp. That feeling is worth a million dollars. Once we get to that point, we feel so much better that we wonder why it took us so long.

Then we can begin to confront our problems logically. We think of one problem on which to begin, and then we might use this formula:

1. What do I want?
2. Is what I'm doing helping me get it?
3. What would I have to change?
4. What's the first step toward making that happen?

A client named Molly had a severe asthma problem which was worsened by cigarette smoke. She judiciously avoided smoky areas and made every attempt to get rid of her condition, even moving her family from New Jersey to Arizona to see if the air here would help.

Indeed it did help, and in a short time Molly was breathing normally. She had a mother-in-law, however, who didn't take her problem very seriously, and when she'd come to visit she smoked as if there were no problem. Molly would cough and wheeze and ask mom-in-law please to smoke outside. But in no time she'd be lighting up again in the house, and Molly would shrug helplessly and look at her husband with plaintive eyes.

Husband would remind Mom not to smoke in the house, Mom would put out her cigarette, and in a few minutes she'd light a new one.

Even the kids got into the act, everyone trying to get the smoker to seek her pleasures on the patio, but to no avail. Molly bought a bronchometer and resigned herself to taking medication when their company was visiting. Needless to say she felt very victimized and resentful and yet helpless because she'd tried to solve the problem and her attempts hadn't worked.

Most of us do the same thing in one way or another. We think of a solution, we try it, and if it doesn't work we try harder. Still doesn't work? We try it harder still.

It's kind of like digging for gold. If I dig a hole and don't find any gold I'll keep digging and digging in that same spot. Eventually I'll be coming out in China but finding no gold. What I have to do is start digging someplace else, and if there's no gold there, perhaps farther over.

Molly's first attempt at a solution was sound: simply explain to Mom and see if she cooperates. No? Okay, then start "digging" someplace else: ask husband to explain. Still no results? How about if the kids try. Zilch response?

Well, then, shall we give up? Only if we want to let ourselves be helpless victims, harboring resentment and damaging our self-esteem.

Molly tried the four steps above.

1. What do I want? I want to breathe easily in a smoke-free home.

2. Is what I'm doing helping me? No.

3. What would I have to change? My mother-in-law's behavior.

4. What's the first step? Changing my own behavior. Asserting myself, stating firmly and respectfully what the rules of the house are.

"Mother Smith, I need to talk to you," Molly began. "My health is badly affected by cigarette smoke, and I can't afford to continue breathing it into my lungs. I'm not willing to have you in the house as long as you smoke here. I'll be happy to call the nearest motel and get you a reservation there if you'd like, or you can quit smoking in the house and stay here. Which would you prefer?"

That was a very difficult conversation for Molly to have. She grew up believing one respected one's elders, especially one's mother-in-law, and this seemed to go against every moral scruple in her body. If she hadn't been so uncomfortable with the smoke, she probably would never have done it.

What's interesting was her mother-in-law's response: "Oh, there's no need to call a motel. I can smoke outside." Which she proceeded to do. And that was that.

Usually people read very clearly the determination and commitment in our manners and voices. All the messages given before had been mild and lacking in commitment, but this time it felt different to both parties. Molly was strong in her determination and it came though.

True, it doesn't always have such good results. Her mother-in-law might have gasped in indignation, stood up and shouted, "You're a wicked, wicked girl, and I regret the day my son married you. I'm leaving your house, all right, and leaving for good! And I hope you burn in hell for being so cruel to a poor old lady."

(It's kind of fun to let ourselves get dramatic as we think of worst-case scenarios!)

While that scene would have been unsettling to Molly, it certainly would have solved the smoke problem. She had to be willing to take that risk when she made the decision to take charge of her life. Unfortunately there is almost always some risk that goes along with taking charge of our lives, and often it's simply someone's disapproval.

So we get to decide: Am I uncomfortable enough to want to change what's happening and take the accompanying risk? Or do I prefer maintaining the status quo and continuing to live in my discomfort? Either way is fine, whichever makes us happier.

There are legions of folks who resign themselves to lifetimes of bad feelings rather than facing the discomfort of a change, and they're not bad or stupid for their choice. Their preference is perfectly acceptable. My concern comes only when those people are unaware of other options they have, so their choice is incomplete.

Many of us have made our decisions simply on the desire to avoid pain, not realizing how much more pain we'll feel staying stuck where we are.

Perhaps it's a process of weighing the amount of pain involved in the decision to change or not to change. Though "pain" might be too strong a word, there is usually some anxiety or apprehension in many of our behavior changes, and that feeling is what scares us into making no change at all.

We say, "Oh, what the heck, I've gotten used to his bad treatment. He'll never change." Or "Why rock the boat? It would just cause bad feelings all around." "I never could stand to have anyone angry at me. I can rise above this and learn not to let it bother me."

What we're really saying is, "I'm too frightened of the scene I might have to face if I assert myself."

It boils down to courage, then. Do I have the courage to move forward even though I'm pretty sure of the bad response I'll get?

On the other hand, do I have enough stamina to stay under this person's thumb for the rest of my life?

The four-step process works beautifully with any kind of problem we want to get rid of, and of course some of the risks we face are frightening. One problem that I encounter with alarming frequency in my office is the spouse who's having an affair. The word "affair" implies another woman or another man, and that's how I'm using it. However, spouses also have other kinds of affairs with jobs, sports, and almost anything else. Those can be just as destructive to a marriage or a relationship.

Holly and Jon were typical examples of two people caught up in the pain of an affair. They came to see me together, both looking sober and sad. Jon had been having an affair with a co-worker for two months, and had admitted it with a lot of relief once Holly confronted him about it. He said he loved Holly very much, as well as their four-year-old daughter, and he didn't want to end the marriage. However, he loved Tricia, too, and it was a more exciting love.

"I feel so young and alive when I'm with Tricia," he explained. "It's not the same kind of love I have for Holly, but my home and family are very important to me, too. I can't imagine losing them. I think I just need some time alone to sort things out."

Holly was crying. "I just can't believe he can do this," she said. "We've had a good marriage up to now. I feel both hurt and angry. A part of me wants to tell him to get the hell out of my house, and the other part wants him to stay. I'm willing to forgive him if he'll give her up now and come back to me. We can work on our marriage. It'll get good again, honey," she said, looking at him hopefully.

Clearly Jon felt uncomfortable at hurting her, but he stayed with his decision to find an apartment of his own "for a while."

It's amazing to me the lengths some wives will go in taking care of their husbands, even in those circumstances. Holly helped him find an apartment and put together boxes of sheets and towels, dishes, pots and silverware. She helped him put the things away in his new kitchen and made up the bed for him.

Her motivation was the hope that he'd see how much she loved him and would come back to her.

Sad to say, it only allowed him to have his cake and eat it too. Jon had the best of both worlds: his nice home and family to go and see, and his exciting lover to grace his freshly made bed in the new place.

Holly continued to see me, poured out her hurt feelings, and read a few books on winning back the one you love. Jon would come by every couple of days to pick up his mail and play with their daughter before going home to the apartment. This went on for weeks, with Jon assuring Holly he was thinking a lot about the whole thing, trying hard to decide what to do. Holly waited patiently and prayed he'd see the light.

Finally she was desperate. (You might guess Jon wasn't.) She sounded defeated when she came for her appointment and looked wrung out. She'd lost fifteen pounds, couldn't sleep, and was understandably depressed.

Throughout that period I'd brought up the four steps and helped her find her options, but it wasn't my place to tell her what to do. I could share my enthusiasm with her, however, when she came in one day looking marvelous. She was different, and it showed in her face and her movements; there was strength now.

"I've suddenly seen what I have to do," she said eagerly, "and it was your four steps that helped. First, what do I want? I want to be happy again. Second, is what I'm doing helping me? No way. I've been miserable. Third, what would I have to change? My behavior! I'm not going to put up with Jon's nonsense any longer. I'm calling a lawyer to start divorce proceedings. He can't have me waiting in the wings while he plays with his bimbo. He's out of my life!

"So the fourth step? I'm telling him so tonight. It's over. He's on his own. I only wish I'd done this sooner."

I was delighted because she was so delighted. She'd stopped waiting for Jon to change and taken the step to change herself. Both of us were eager to see what Jon would do with this information, and what he did was a very common response.

Jon called me for an appointment the next day and came in looking shaken. "I don't know what happened to Holly," he said, "but all of a sudden she wants a divorce. I don't see how she can make a decision like that so quickly. I mean, think what that's going to do to our little girl!"

"It'll be tough for her," I agreed.

"I mean, hell, can't we have some time to see if we can work this thing out?" he complained.

"Boy, I don't know," I said honestly. "Holly just got tired of waiting for you to decide between her and Tricia. But if you don't want the divorce, now's the time to tell her so. I know she loves you. Who knows, maybe it's not too late to save the marriage if that's what you want."

Long story short: he did and they did. The catalyst was Holly's decision to take back her power, no longer depending on Jon to come around to her way of thinking. It's true that we teach people how we will be treated, and she'd made the mistake of teaching him he could treat her badly. Now she simply had to teach a different message: I'm worthwhile, and I refuse to stay married to you if you're unfaithful.

Of course there was a risk. Holly had to be prepared for Jon to say, "Fine with me, go ahead and file. Let's get this divorce on the road." She'd decided that such a response would be preferable to living in their present state, and once she knew she could handle that she was on the right track.

There's no way of knowing in advance how the other person is going to respond, and we can't make our decisions based on game playing or an attempt to manipulate. Had Holly thought, "I know. I'll shake him up by saying I want a divorce and then he'll come back to me," she might have been very disappointed. She had to resolve within herself that she was strong in her own right and that she could handle being single again, and to believe it would be preferable to sharing Jon with another woman.

With that resolution she was ready to deal with his next move.

It is that kind of risk, however, that makes people stay stuck in situations that are making them miserable. It's said, "Better the devil you know than the devil you don't know." So often we continue to live in really rotten circumstances because we're too afraid to face that unknown factor. And that's our choice…or one of our choices.

Usually we have many options available to us. In this case Holly had three obvious ones:

1. Maintain the status quo, letting Jon stay home with her while he carried on his affair with Tricia.

2. Continue being married to him after he'd moved to his own apartment.

3. Refuse to remain his wife since he wasn't honoring his marriage vows.

Every problem we have presents more than one option to us, and yet often it's hard to see more than one. That's why it's helpful to talk to others about it, because they generally see the picture differently than we who are emotionally involved.

The danger in listening to others' advice, however, is their particular bias about the issue. Friends and family members may have vested interests in seeing us act one way or another, and we might let ourselves be influenced by their opinions. Then we're turning over our power to still another source instead of using it to make the best decision for ourselves.

A client of mine whose wife is cheating on him quotes his parents: "My folks say I must stay married for the sake of the kids. They need both parents in order to grow up happy and well adjusted."

While ideally all children would have two loving parents who provide the warm, supportive atmosphere in which to learn about life, many times that just isn't happening. Unless the two parents love each other as well as their kids, they're probably going to set a pretty sorry example of what a family can be.

But that certainly doesn't mean they should junk the marriage! There are other avenues to explore which may improve it. I believe there isn't a married couple alive who at some time hasn't gritted their teeth and rued the day of their wedding. We all have times when we think our marriage was a big mistake. It's the hardest challenge we face, in my estimation, but one most of us are able to work through. However, we need to be aware of all the problem-solving skills available to us.

The four steps are excellent for resolving all kinds of difficulties within the context of marriage and any other relationship. Let's look at another example.

Trying to lose weight, that's practically a universal problem. Suppose I've been counting calories for months now and haven't gotten anywhere. Maybe I lose a pound or two, and then I gain it back. A hefty friend of ours used to brag, "I've lost a ton of weight, literally." Every year for the last forty years he'd lost fifty pounds and then gained them back. While I suspect he exaggerated, most of us are aware of the yo-yo syndrome.

Okay, let's apply our four steps.

1. What do I want? To be slender.
2. Is what I'm doing helping me? No.
3. What would I have to change? My method. Counting calories is not working for me. I need a different system.
4. What's the first step?

There could be any number of possible first steps. Calling Overeaters Anonymous or Weight Watchers or one of the commercial weight loss centers. Going to the library or bookstore for information on how to lose weight. Talking to friends who've gotten thinner about what worked for them. Making an appointment with a doctor or a counselor, and perhaps getting a referral to one who specializes in weight loss.

Then we need to choose the one we want to be our first step in this experience. It may not be the one that works for us, either. Maybe we'll go through all the methods above plus thirty more before we hit on the technique that works for us. But isn't it wonderful to have so many options?

Our mistake comes only in thinking we're failures just because we haven't succeeded so far. Actually all those "failures" have just shown us what doesn't work so we don't have to waste any more time on those options. We're free to go on and try something new, whatever we want that to be.

thirteen

Intimacy and Beliefs

We attended a lovely wedding about a year ago, and I ran into the bride recently buying groceries. We hugged and laughed in our excitement at seeing each other, and I asked eagerly, "How's married life?"

She clouded. "The truth?" she asked.

"Of course," I insisted.

"Lee, I think my husband needs to go back in the oven. He's not done yet."

We sat on a bench and talked for a while, and I lamented that men are not as simple as cookies or muffins. They could go back in the oven for months or years, and they would never get any more "done." We really have to take them as they are. "Ready or not, here we come."

I know, of course, that we women are not done, either, and our mates have to patiently work with us while we're working with them.

We got married for the wrong reasons, anyway: sexual attraction and unrealistic views of how much our partners would love us and care for us and want to be with us.

If we stay married long enough we end up closer to the "right" reasons: love that includes physical affection as well as appreciation of each other's strengths, awareness and acceptance of one another's weaknesses, the desire to be helpful, supportive, to spend quality time together, to be each other's helpmates and soul mates.

But nowhere is it written that we'll agree on everything. We'll see things differently, and we'll each have interests that the other finds dull as dirt. We begin to look different from the way we looked when we first fell in love. Some of our values will have changed, some matching more closely those of our mates, and others vastly different.

Sometimes we look at the other person and wonder, "Now, why was it that I chose this mate?"

Ironically, the things that attracted us most in the first place become the things that now drive us crazy.

In our courting days I thought Larry was endearingly precious when he proclaimed, "Just looking at a hammer gives me a headache." Nowadays I don't think it's a bit cute when I see his reluctance to fix anything that needs tools.

He loved my nurturing and clinginess. After a few years of marriage he found it too confining, and he distanced himself.

I used to be impressed at his sociability and all the many activities in which he was involved. Now I resent them because the bulk of his time is spent at meetings.

He used to be impressed at my piano performing, but later when I played in piano bars he resented my friendliness with men, even though I was just as friendly with the women.

How in the world can we keep a relationship alive when our mates disappoint us? That's a tremendous challenge to anyone who's ever married, I suspect, and it's one of the reasons so many people choose to live together without marriage. It's way easier to get out when the disappointments come.

Many people have a strong fear of commitment—men and women. Some of us fear commitment of any description, even a party invitation or a planned vacation. Those who feel reluctant about even committing to an evening may feel almost phobic about a lifetime commitment.

It was simpler in the olden days. When the vast majority of women refused to have sex until they had the wedding ring, men knew if they wanted sex they'd better propose. Sex is a strong motivator, as we all know.

But since sex is more generously given among many people today, the men feel no urgency to make The Commitment. Neither do the women, at first, but usually they begin to hanker for permanence, unless they're older and quite independent anyway. Then they may even prefer the arrangement of a live-in lover with the freedom to kick him out if they tire of him.

I'm not making a moral judgment here, but simply reporting what goes on in most of the world, no secret to any of us anyway.

In both marriage and in a live-in relationship we generally notice that sex loses some of its luster after it's been experienced enough times. And what's "enough?" That varies, of course. "Enough" hits the women first, and often doesn't hit the man at all.

Couples who come for counseling almost universally complain that sex is a problem. "How could that be?" they ask. "It used to be the highlight of our life!"

I tell them, "It's just one form of communication, and a good thermometer to indicate how the relationship itself is measuring up." If the sex is frequent and fun, the marriage is generally a strong one.

If sex is a frequent problem there needs to be some digging to find the weaknesses between the couple. Good sex can't return until both people feel loved and respected.

When either party gets too busy with other interests to spend much time in togetherness, then you can predict a dramatic drop in sex.

A good truth to remember is: Our feelings go where our energy goes.

Often one or both parties make their careers their first priority. Naturally their feelings will go there, too. Their jobs become their "mates," and the couple relationship diminishes.

Mothers can actually fall in love with their babies, and all their energy and feelings go in that direction. It's natural for husbands to feel shut out when that happens.

But whatever the problems, they can be rooted out and discussed and eventually solved, if both parties want the relationship to work. If only one wants to put forth the effort it's the beginning of the end. The end of the love, not necessarily the end of the relationship.

We all know couples who have been married for years and years, but who seem to have stopped loving one another long ago. They stay together for financial reasons or moral issues, or whatever their particular beliefs dictate, but the love is long gone. It's become simply a living arrangement that fills some needs in both of them.

There's nothing inherently wrong with that, but it's sure not a relationship of intimacy.

So we need to be aware of where our energy is going, and if it isn't going toward the relationship we must either redirect our energy or be honest about our priorities.

One man turned to his wife halfway through their session and said, "Honey, all I want is for you to make me feel like the counselor makes me feel. She understands and accepts and empathizes. Why can't you do that?"

I quickly explained that I have no emotional investment in their permanent relationship, so I can see their problems and possible solutions clearly. I don't *need* anything from either one, which sows how dependency complicates our lives tremendously.

If I'm the party who hungers for intimate and tender conversation to feed the flame of desire, I'll be focused on that loss. If I'm the party who hungers for more physical sex, I'll be focused on that loss.

It's commonly said that women use sex to get love and men use love to get sex—which seems to be true, but isn't always the case. I've had women clients who wish their husbands would want more frequent sex, and men with the same complaint about their wives.

I remember one client whose complaint was that her husband never seemed to want sex. He didn't know why either, but he didn't. They were deciding to divorce, and I didn't see them anymore.

But I ran into the husband at the airport a couple of years later, and he was married to someone else. "I don't know why," he said, "but now I can't get enough sex and the new wife doesn't want to very often."

We shared a laugh at the irony of the situation, and his plane was boarding so that was all the time we had.

Looking through Glommer Glasses, the glommer would probably be all over the non-glommer like a rash if the tender caring were present. The non-glommer would enjoy all the sexual activity available with or without much tender caring.

Again the question: Is either party right or wrong? Again the answer: No.

Like so many relationship problems, there is not an easy "one-size-fits-all" solution. Surprisingly, perhaps, I often compare marriage to any business relationship. It can't run smoothly without respectful communication, flexibility, and compromise.

Glommer or non-glommer, sex is often a joyous event even when it's scheduled. I know we don't like that fact. We'd much rather it be spontaneous and wonderful, when the whim presents itself, like when we were young and carefree.

Like everything else about us, sex can always be improved upon, starting simply with conversation.

Parents of young children today often tell their little ones to "Use your words, sweetie."

Life would be so much simpler if we all used our words instead of trying to manipulate others with our feelings, our body language, and our behavior.

The Final Solution

When all is said and done I'm still a glommer. You're still whatever you were before you read this book. Let's sum it up.

We are who we are: some of it born into us in our DNA, some of it in the decisions we made in our childhood. Some is due to experiences, from marvelous to traumatic, that happened to us along the way and markedly changed our early decisions.

We are conglomerations of many facets, physical and mental, emotional and spiritual, the combinations of which make us unique. Sometimes we like the cards we were dealt, sometimes not.

Most of us wish other people would make some changes in order to make us happier. But for most of us, that just does not happen.

It would appear, then, that we're stuck.

But, oh, we are so *not* stuck!

We have loads of power with which to change our lives, our expectations, our intentions, our hopes, wishes, grudges, fears and dreams.

Alfred Adler used to tell people to picture the huge power of a waterfall made by nature (or God). The mighty roar it makes awes us and can almost overwhelm us.

Or watch a forest fire with its tremendous power going full speed ahead as it destroys thousands of trees and acres of property.

Enjoy seeing giant waves wash upon a shore. Watch the brilliant displays of lightning and hear the mighty cracks of thunder.

All are samples of nature's God-given power.

You and I don't have the kind of breathtaking, tangible, forceful power that destroys forests and villages, but we do have amazingly strong control over our own minds when we choose to exercise it. We have the commanding determination needed to change our thinking and adjust our behavior in order to change our troubled lives.

God gave us that power. If we're heavy-hearted about a particular situation that we've resented for a very long time, we *do* have the power to change it, and if we haven't done that it's because we're not willing to pay the price.

One of our kids came home from an economics class years ago with a story told by the professor.

"Once upon a time all the most brilliant people in the world got together to discuss life and philosophy. They wanted to find a way to educate the masses on the most important information in the world."

They labored diligently, writing thousands of pages of information into some dozens of books, but when they had it all written they realized it was way too much material for people to read. Nobody had that much time for reading, so they decided to condense it all into one big book.

After months of study they had done it. All the important facts were in one huge volume. Then they saw that that wasn't the solution; it was still much too long.

Again they labored until it was down to one chapter. Still too wordy. Weeks later they had it down to one page at which they stared diligently before shaking their heads.

Knowing then that it must be condensed to one simple sentence, they worked day and night until they agreed on the necessary words.

The most important information known to mankind is "There is no such thing as a free lunch."

Nothing is free. We pay some kind of price for every single thing we eat and drink and wear. Every kind of entertainment and medical care. Every sport, luxury, travel and education. A price for getting married, for divorcing, for dying. For a beautiful garden and a clean house, both costing us time and energy if not money.

When, frequently, we haven't the means to pay for something we want, then we must do without it.

The decisions we make don't cost us, but acting on them does. If I'm unhappy I'm generally resisting paying the price it would cost to achieve or acquire what I want. "The price" is usually not about money, but on circumstances which affect our lives.

It boils down, then, to our choosing whichever option is the *least* disagreeable to us, perhaps understanding that many of our choices will bring us some amount of unhappiness.

We must figuratively weigh them on scales like the butcher weighs the pork roast.

I may really want a nice big tenderloin of beef, but a pound of hamburger is all I can afford. Most of us don't stand there in the market wishing the tenderloin were cheaper. We don't tell off the butcher for requiring that much money. We see the numbers, we buy our ground beef and home we go.

Dealing with what makes us unhappy in life is exactly the same principle: we need/get to decide which price we can afford and accept it. If we do that we're generally content, or at least not in pain.

If we continue resenting having to eat hamburgers instead of steak we're *un*happy.

I'm a glommer, keenly aware for some 60 years that my husband is just the opposite. Every single time I visit that disappointment (frustration, regret, anger, sadness, bitterness; call it what you will) I am making myself unhappy. Larry isn't making me unhappy. He's going about town to his meetings quite happily, not bothering me one bit. He isn't even resenting me.

Only I am making myself unhappy wishing I had steak instead. Wasting precious time playing a sick game of mental solitaire. I've played it hundreds of times, none of which have done one thing toward making me happy but only more unhappy.

Am I crazy?

No, just normal. We all do it.

We really resist letting go of a strong desire even though we'd be happier if we did. Some folks say, "Better the devil I know than the devil I don't know."

But regardless of what our problems are, we virtually always can change our thinking, and that results in relief. Once I change my thinking from "Oh me oh my, I wish wish *wish* I had an attentive husband so life would be the way I dreamed it would be" to "I have a husband who is a good guy; honest and sober and generous," I'm halfway to the next sentence which is, "Isn't it nice I can make myself happy!"

I do live a happy life filled with activities I enjoy, and I've realized that I might not be that way if Larry had been more attentive. I know that I've always loved music and drama. When I went to college I minored in drama and joined the Shrine of Ages Choir which was well known in Arizona for singing on Easter as the sun rose over the Grand Canyon. We also took a two-state tour every spring, so it took a lot of practice time. I also got a part in the first play.

Ah, but that was before I met Eddie. I so loved him that I quit both activities so I could spend most of my leisure time being with him.

Had Larry been the least bit glomming I'd have sat beside him happily reveling in his company. Which sounds nice to me right now, but I'd never have achieved the various roles I've savored in music and education.

I have a good friend, a glommer who is married to a glommer, and she tells him joyfully as they walk along the beach holding hands, "I'm your little barnacle." I envy her.

But would I be content if Larry were the main source of my fun activities? I seriously doubt it. What I want is the best of both worlds. Can't have both? Then I can certainly fill my spare time with the other kinds of fun I've pursued.

Sadly, too many of us tend to focus on what's missing in our lives instead of what we have, and I must plead guilty. Knowing that, though, I can continue focusing on enjoying what I have instead of regretting what I don't have.

That's true for all of us, whatever our issues are. Instead of going back over them time and again, we can change our thoughts. It's difficult to change our feelings, but by changing our thoughts our feelings will usually change.

There is a little three-step formula that I first heard from Dr. William Glasser which explains how feelings form. Let's say there is an action that happens. Okay, the action is represented by the letter A.

- ACTION: I'm going for a walk in the neighborhood when I see a dog crossing the street ahead of me.

- Let's say that I have a BELIEF about dogs the my mother taught me when I was six. "Dogs are dangerous. You never know whether they bite people or not. Better avoid them at all costs."

If that is my belief, my C (CONSEQUENTIAL FEELING) at seeing the approaching dog will be fear.

If your belief is "Dogs are loving little critters who are usually friendly and glad to see you, so don't be afraid of them," you'll see the dog approaching with a vastly different consequential feeling. You'll be eager to see the little guy. Not a trace of fear will you feel.

So it's not the Action which makes you feel afraid, but your Belief that danger lies ahead.

Such is true in everything we observe in life.

There's a massive monsoon storm approaching, common in Tucson summers. Action: Storm coming.

If my Belief is "Storms are dangerous and lightning might kill me," I'm going to feel extremely frightened as I watched that storm move in.

If your B belief is "Yay! There's nothing so awesome as a monsoon storm, and Tucson certainly needs the rain!" then your Consequential feeling is sheer delight at the approaching storm.

Again, our feelings stem from our beliefs.

Therefore we need to examine our belief systems and figure out what belief is causing our emotional turmoil.

A glommer would harbor the long-nurtured belief that "When someone loves you they should want to spend lots of time with you, talking and showing you affection."

When the glommer's partner comes home from work, the glommer would be expecting a cozy chat, some affection and appreciation, some laughter and physical contact.

So if (A) the non-glomming partner comes home with a quick kiss on the cheek, a beer, and turning on the TV, the glommer partner thinks (B), "Well, what's wrong? What's wrong with our marriage? Why doesn't he love me? Clearly he likes TV better than me." The glommer then feels (C) sad and disappointed.

If that's a pattern in the relationship, the glommer needs to change his/her belief to: "When my partner comes home from work s/he needs time to veg out, enjoy a beer and a TV show," there is no resulting pain. Amazing! It's that simple.

Except it isn't. Remember the price factor, how we're unwilling to pay the price?

If I change my belief to the one above, I'm giving up a lifelong view of what makes a happy marriage. I convince myself that my partner is ruining our marriage, from what could have been a swell one to one that's rotten to the core.

I don't want to let go of that belief. It's how life should *be*, for crying out loud! If I let go of that belief (and the resulting punishment I give my partner) I'm encouraging an unhappy marriage. I can't do that. You can't expect me to do that! It's too big a price to pay!

And that's what keeps us stuck.

I said "There's always a price to pay for anything we want."

We need to check out our goals first. What is it that I want? I'd usually say, "A happy, close, intimate relationship."

Okay, what are you doing to try to achieve that?"

"Well, I'm reminding my partner that he should be more talkative and desirous of close, intimate contacts."

"Okay, is it working?"

"No!"

"How would you change your belief in order to make yourself happy?

"Well, I'd have to give up that lifelong dream and find some way to entertain myself after he comes home from work."

"Okay. Are you willing to do that?"

"No *way*!"

And thus the problem remains, along with the unhappiness (probably in both parties).

Of course a lot of couples file for divorce then, thinking they might as well as be single if marriage is going to be that non-affectionate and non-close.

The thing is, then they each have to seek out new partners or remain single, and both those options bring out new problems with which to deal. New problems which make us wish the other person would change. Again. And the other person won't. Again.

So once more we have to learn how to be happy on our own.

Learning this is unquestionably a nuisance, especially when all we're wanting is for the other person to make the changes, but it's *so* worth it. Once we master that skill, no matter how long it takes us, we have the capacity to be relatively happy for the rest of our lives regardless of what problems we encounter. That's worth a hundred million dollars right there!

fourteen

How Quickly Can I Make These Changes?

The answer depends on how unhappy you are. Generally we won't bother to change ourselves unless we're *really* unhappy. If we're pretty much just disgusted, we won't want to work that hard to change.

If we're reluctant to "let the partner off the hook" (as I was in the interview with Tom Condon), we aren't willing to allow that to happen. We insist on remaining miserable in order to continue punishing the errant mate. God forbid we become happy and the partner doesn't feel punished anymore!

Most of us want that rotten son-of-a-bitch to see, daily, hourly, how hurt/angry/suffering we are, and that it's all *his* or *her* fault! I mean, yeah, I'm miserable, but it's worth it if I can keep my idiot mate miserable, too. That's a huge payoff for me.

Give that up? When donkeys fly.

It's only when we're so *very* miserable, with enormous amounts of pain torturing us almost constantly, that we finally can reach the point of being ready to change ourselves.

What do we change first? Our expectation. We have to let go of the wish that our partner will suddenly hit himself in the forehead and say, "Ah, I get it! I'm a jerk, sure enough! My poor partner has suffered nobly for these many years, and it's all been my fault. I'm a rotten, selfish loser is what I am! Suddenly I see the truth and will spend the rest of my life trying to make it up to her/him. I'm a changed person as of now."

Doesn't that sound wonderful, fellow suffering mates? Wouldn't we love to hear those words?

Are you telling me I have to give up that dream? *Nooo*! It isn't *fair*!

And you may be 100% correct. It's possible it *is* all your mate's fault, and s/he doesn't deserve to be released from your skillful, well-practiced punishment. But we're not talking about your partner right now. We're talking about us. *You*! Happiness, yours and mine. Don't *we* deserve to be happy?

Darned right we do.

So why do we have to forgive and forget and let our errant partners *be*?

Because we want to feel better, is why. We want to be happy. And the only way we can achieve that state is by letting our partners off the hook and turning our focus onto ourselves—our beliefs and expectations. We're the important ones here.

We might compare the process to a person who's been injured some way, like badly burned in a fire. The person is now a patient in an intensive care unit. S/he is going to live, but it will require some months of painful therapy.

Every day the patient will have to endure treatments that cause pain and anxiety, anger and fear. Is it worth it? Yes, because when the treatments are over the patient will walk out of the hospital healed and happy again.

Can't I have that without the agony? Nope. You can't. The agony is what assures the happiness.

Keep in mind, you can refuse the agony and continue living the life of pain you've endured for lo these many years. But if you want to be freed of the agony you simply *must* endure the painful treatments.

Yes or no? No or yes? Yes or no? We get to decide.

"Well, hmmmm. I guess no."

Okay. You're back on your own, living with this undeserving, insensitive jerk. You hate it; you hate him or her.

Bye now. Have a nice life.

"What? My life will *not* be nice! I hate my life!"

Oh, well, do you want to change your mind and go through the therapy, pain and disappointment, and all?

Silence.

"Oh, okay. I guess so."

Okey-dokey. Your homework is to let go of thinking about what a jerk your mate is. When that thought occurs to you and you realize it, you say to yourself, "No. I don't want to go there."

And you find some other subject on which to focus. You might bake some cinnamon rolls. Or answer e-mails. Take a shower. Call a sick friend. Clean the bathroom. Go grocery shopping. Dust mop. Find a few clothes to give to the Salvation Army.

And if you find yourself thinking about The Jerk you say, "Stop!" and immediately think of something else. The stars you read about in People Magazine. The TV listings. Whether or not you want to take a class in social dancing at the city park. Painting an end table. Fixing yourself a sandwich for lunch.

It's not an easy process. And if you'd like some little mini-breaks, try this: Decide how many minutes you want to feel miserable again. Total for the whole day? How about 20 minutes a day? Okay, you can have them all at once or a portion of them every hour or two. You get to decide.

I love that phrase, "I get to decide." It reminds me I have the power here. Nobody can make me suffer if I don't want to."

You might decide to suffer for four minutes five times a day. Choose the times. How about:
- Four minutes in my morning shower.
- Four minutes driving to work.
- Another four driving to lunch.
- Four more while fixing dinner.
- And the final four while cleaning up after dinner.

There now, you've done it! You've done your whole day's worth of suffering easy as pie. During those allotted four-minute periods you've kept yourself focusing totally on The Jerk's rotten behavior. And now you're free for the rest of the day.

You get to spend your evening any way you like, except for suffering. Should a bit of suffering occur to you, you immediately say, "No!" and think of another subject.

I promise you this works. I've done it myself more than a few times.

Gradually you can lessen the suffering time to 16 minutes a day, then ten minutes a day. Finally no minutes a day. You know you won't fall victim to further remembering what a jerk the jerk *is*. It's his/her problem, not yours. You're too busy thinking of fun things you can do. Why would you waste your precious time focusing on his/her jerk-ness?

You're past that. Been there, done that. No fun. Not worth it. Bye-bye suffering. Hello, fun!

I enjoy telling the joke about two contractors who eat their lunch together every day. On Monday Frank opens up his sandwich and grins, saying, "Oh, man, I got a liverwurst on rye! My favorite sandwich!"

His friend, Orville, opens his and says grimly, "I got a cheese sandwich."

On Tuesday Frank opens his and beams as he says, "Aye! I have pastrami on pumpernickel. I love it!"

Orville glumly says, "I got a cheese sandwich."

On Wednesday Frank shouts, "Yay! I got roast beef with horseradish on sourdough! This is my favorite!"

Orville mutters, "I got a cheese sandwich."

Frank says with a little annoyance, "Why don't you tell your wife you don't like cheese sandwiches?"

Orville says, "Hey, leave my wife out of this. I make my own lunch!"

Funny, yeah. But it describes many of us who continue to put up with behavior we dislike, and yet we're unwilling to change whatever we must in order to be happy. And we often get to keep blaming the other person.

One of my friends has been waiting for 45 years for her husband to give her a Valentine gift. Every year she complains about the fact that it didn't happen.

You probably know what my advice to her was: "This year you buy yourself a Valentine gift. Anything you want!"

The nicest thing about this method of changing our own behavior is that it works in every area of our lives. Many of them have nuisance qualities about them, right? At least mine do.

And it can be actually fun to try to think of the options we have when we're, say, standing in line at Walmart, as I was today. I joined a line in which the two people ahead of me were having all sorts of problems, and the rest of us stood there *forever* waiting for them to get solved.

Other Walmart employees were called over, and they would all read sales slips and converse with one another and then call a different manager, who would join them in their confusion.

Making it worse was a furious guy behind me who kept shouting, "Hey, let's get this line going, people! We've been waiting forever. What the hell is going on? We should have been out of here 30 minutes ago!"

At first I hadn't been in a hurry, but as other lines finished up and ours was still busily trying to solve the problems, it was getting tiresome to all of us.

I began to think of my options. Obviously I couldn't change the behavior of the Walmart employees *or* their customers. I realized if I was unhappy I had to change my position somehow.

I looked at other lines, some of which were "do it yourself" lines, which I hate. Didn't want to go there. Others were even longer than mine. I could, of course, walk out, leaving my basket of refried beans behind, but I wanted those for dinner tonight.

I could yell at the offending duo who were causing the problem, but I knew they weren't going to leave until their difficulty was solved.

I could call for management, but clearly they were already there and helpless in making everything okay.

After going through my options I knew I could do nothing but wait in line.

Still I had options. I could wait feeling furious like the man behind me. I could burst into tears and wail loudly to release my frustrations. Or I could stand quietly and patiently, letting my mind wander to pleasant places I'd been or to which I planned to go. I chose that option. It was *my* choice. I was in charge of me; nobody else was.

After about 20 minutes the problems got solved and the rest of us got checked out. I wondered how the man behind me felt. I'm guessing he stayed furious for a long time, poor guy.

It was certainly not an ideal situation, but it's common and normal. Life is so full of irritating moments, but they go with the territory.

Glommer and non-glommers alike experience all those nuisance moments, and both have the ability of choosing our favorite option.

When our son Lyle was around four he would come into the house and ask whoever he found first, "Would you rather be run over by a garbage truck or eaten by a hippopotamus?" Or some similar question.

Frequently our options are like that: dilemmas with two or more lousy choices. Everybody's are. And then all we can do is choose the one which is least awful.

I guess I'd take the run-over-by-a-garbage-truck over getting eaten by a hippo. Thank goodness our real options are usually not that horrible.

So whatever our problems are, glommers and non-glommers, many of them have nothing to do with our glom quotient. They have more to do with the tedious annoyances everyone faces. Co-workers who talk too loudly or have bad breath. Kids in restaurants who make all the diners crazy with their noisy escapades. Neighbors who play loud music on late night weekend parties. Dogs who bark endlessly all night long. Drivers who cut us off in traffic.

Committed partners who ignore us or are sarcastic and disrespectful. People who let their dogs poop on our front lawns and leave it there. Teenagers who worry us to death by not coming home at the appointed time. Strangers who dent our cars in parking lots and leave no phone numbers. Bosses who don't give us the raises we deserve. Preachers who talk too long. Neighbors who talk too long. Party guests who whisper secrets to each other. Store clerks who talk on the phone instead of waiting on people trying to buy something.

Once we accept the truth that we cannot change those people, we can begin to solve our problems in other ways. Some, of course, are serious and need to be turned over to the law. Sometimes we even have to move to a different house or neighborhood to protect ourselves from harm.

But it's always up to us to take back our power and make changes happen, even though they don't always make us happy. If they improve our lives somewhat, however, that may be the best we can expect.

Life is hard. Nowhere was it ever chiseled in stone that life would be easy. We just think it should be.

It is said that centuries ago a king demanded that his kingdom be covered in leather so he could walk barefoot without getting thorns in his feet. One of his subjects suggested, "Your highness, may we just cover your feet in leather so you can walk anyplace and not step on thorns?" Thus shoes were invented.

We need to make sure we are taking care of ourselves and our needs. Glommers and non-glommers alike, we make our own lunches!

Acknowledgments

I am so fortunate to have a lab in my very own family. Our two daughters, Laurie and Lisa, discovered the categories of glommers and non-glommers, and they shared their beliefs with me. They've always been fascinated partners in investigating and understanding relationships.

Our two sons, Lindsay and Lyle, listen to me patiently as I expound on all my insights, thoughts, hopes, dreams and fears, with kindness hiding their probable indifference, which I appreciate mightily.

I'm so lucky to have their spouses, Pete, Tom, Nancy and Nanci, whose love I feel all the time, even though they may sometimes be a bit disinterested in my ramblings. They never show it, and I love them for it.

Among all of them are various degrees of glomming and non-glomming, and I enjoy watching them work around their DNA tendencies in order to sustain truly rich, contented marriages. I find myself always learning from their examples.

I'm blessed, too, in having Larry for a husband. Coming from a courtship during which we thought we were "exactly alike," we've uncovered way more differences than similarities, most of which have caused some disappointment on both sides. But we stay united, recognizing the respect and love we have for one another after 60 years of marriage, knowing the other is there for us when we need them. Always we trust one another.

Our three grandchildren—Christopher, Sedona and Rye—are getting to experience all the gifts and problems everyone encounters as young adults, and they bound forward eagerly to conquer each challenge. I'm so proud to be their "grammy." They're the frosting on the cake.

About the Author

Lee was born Leona Marie Koenig on Aug. 22, 1932—a Depression baby—in Williams, AZ. Her brother Paul was three years older. Their mother stayed home to care for them and their father was a stenographer for the Santa Fe Railroad, so the family was transferred all along the Santa Fe line from Williams to Ash Fork to Winslow to Los Angeles and back again.

In L.A. Paul took up the saxophone, and Leona the piano. For one year she took lessons from a teenager who charged fifty cents a lesson, but when they moved to Winslow her training ended. It was a good thing, though, because she discovered she could play by ear. She and Paul played at a new teen club, "The Welcome On Inn," and then in nightclubs. Though she was only 15, her parents never worried if Leona was with her brother.

The piano became her road to many stages of life. She played for dances with the college jazz band in

Flagstaff and got her first radio show there. That's where she met her future husband, Larry, a radio announcer who called her "Lee," which stuck. After graduating from Arizona State College she moved to Tucson as a first-grade teacher and landed another radio show on the side. She and Larry married in Winslow in June, 1953.

His job as a DJ took them to Phoenix and then Tucson, where Lee resumed teaching until their four children joined them. While mothering Laurie, Lisa, Lindsay and Lyle, she formed a band that played for parties and receptions, and taught piano to beginning students.

At forty she returned to college, this time the University of Arizona, for a master's degree in counseling and guidance. As a marriage and family therapist she wrote three self-help books and presented at conferences internationally. She retired at 75 and started The Star-Spangled Seniors, a group of 22 singers who perform at no cost for nursing and assisted living homes. Read about them at xgboy.com/html/sssindex.html.

Additional Books By Lee Schnebly:

<u>Out of Apples</u>

<u>Do-It-Yourself Happiness</u>

<u>I Do?</u>

<u>Nurturing Yourself and Others</u>

<u>Being Happy Being Married</u>

<u>The Best of Both Worlds</u>

www.ingramcontent.com/pod-product-compliance
Lightning Source LLC
Chambersburg PA
CBHW061637040426
42446CB00010B/1462